MARY,
STAR OF
THE NEW
MILLENNIUM

Andrew Ganne
Feb. '01

MARY, STAR OF THE NEW MILLENNIUM

Guiding Us to Renewal

DAVID E. ROSAGE

CHARIS

SERVANT PUBLICATIONS
ANN ARBOR, MICHIGAN

Charis Books is an imprint of Servant Publications especially designed to serve Roman Catholics.

Unless otherwise indicated Scripture quotes are from the Revised Standard Version of the Bible, © 1946, 1952, 1971 by the Division of Christian Education of the National Council of Churches of Christ in the USA. Used by permission. Verses marked NRSV are from the Revised Standard Version of the Bible, © 1989 by the Division of Christian Education of the National Council of Churches of Christ in the USA. Used by permission. All rights reserved. Verses marked NAB are from the NEW AMERICAN BIBLE, © 1970 by the Confraternity of Christian Doctrine, Washington, D.C. All rights reserved.

Published by Servant Publications
P.O. Box 8617
Ann Arbor, Michigan 48107

Cover design: Hile Illustration and Design, Ann Arbor, Michigan

97 98 99 00 10 9 8 7 6 5 4 3 2

Printed in the United States of America
ISBN 0-89283-994-5

Library of Congress Cataloging-in-Publication Data

Rosage, David E.
Mary, star of the new millennium : guiding us to renewal / David E. Rosage.
    p.   cm.
Includes bibliographical references.
ISBN 0-89283-994-5
1. Mary, Blessed Virgin, Saint.   2. Mary, Blessed Virgin, Saint—Apparitions and miracles.   3. Mary, Blessed Virgin, Saint—Theology.   4. Spiritual life—Catholic Church.
5. Catholic Church—Doctrines.   I. Title.
BT602.R66   1997
232.91—dc21

This volume is dedicated
to all people who,
with Mary's guidance,
are striving to bring to fruition
the objectives of the millennial renewal
in their own lives
and
in the lives of everyone they touch.

CONTENTS

Introduction / 11

Part One:
Messages from Mary to the Modern-Day Church / 17
1. Mary, Guiding Star of the New Millennium / 19
2. Guadalupe: A Call to Build a Community of Faith / 31
3. Lourdes: A Call to Healing and Holiness / 39
4. Fatima: A Call to Prayer and Commitment / 51
5. Medjugorje: A Call to the Sacramental Life / 61
6. Mary, Mother of the Church / 69

Part Two:
Lessons from the Life of Mary / 81
7. Mary: Model of Discernment and Obedience / 83
   The Early Life of Mary Through the Annunciation
8. Mary: Model of Prayer / 97
   The Visitation and the Birth of Jesus
9. Mary: Model of Faith and Hope / 113
   The Early Life and Ministry of Jesus
10. Mary: Model of Suffering / 129
    The Passion and Death of Christ
11. Mary: Model of Discipleship / 141
    The Resurrection Through Pentecost
12. Mary: Queen of Peace / 161
    The Assumption and Intercession of Mary

Epilogue / 183

ACKNOWLEDGEMENTS

I am deeply grateful to:

Sister Mary Jean Meyer, O.P., for compiling voluminous notes into a systematic resource and for an ongoing critique in the development of the manuscript,

Anna Cullis for many important suggestions and for a critical appraisal of the manuscript in preparation for the final draft,

Maxine Keogh for laboriously deciphering and preparing the various drafts, for valuable recommendations, and for typing and retyping the manuscript in its final form.

INTRODUCTION

IN THE APOSTOLIC LETTER "The Coming of the Third Millennium," Pope John Paul II declares that the years 1997-1999 are to be a Church-wide time of preparation for the third millennium. In this letter, the Holy Father emphasizes the importance of the Mother of God in this three-phased endeavor:

> *The Blessed Virgin,* who will be as it were "indirectly" present in the whole preparatory phase, will be contemplated in this first year especially in the mystery of her Divine Motherhood. It was in her womb that the Word became flesh! The affirmation of the central place of Christ cannot therefore be separated from the recognition of the role played by his Most Holy Mother.[1]

In *Mary, Star of the New Millennium,* we will consider both Mary's example in the Gospels and the important and powerful role she plays in the Great Renewal. As we prayerfully ponder the supreme mystery of the Incarnation, we will be blessed with a deeper appreciation of God's infinite love in sending his Son, Jesus, as our Savior and Redeemer. We will be touched by Mary's willingness to fulfill her role, not only in the mystery of the Incarnation, but in whatever the Lord asked of her throughout her whole life.

Three Phases of Renewal

There are three major phases outlined by the Holy Father for entering wholeheartedly into the process of renewing and revitalizing our Christian way of life as we approach the third millennium.

Growing in Faith in Jesus. According to the proclamation of the Holy Father, 1997 will mark the first phase of our preparations. During this time we are called to contemplate the Person of Jesus and his centrality in our daily living. For a thorough treatment of this subject, you might find it helpful to read my book *Rekindle Your Love for Jesus* (Servant, 1996).

We need to know Jesus as a caring, concerned, personal God who loves us as much as the Father loves him (see Jn 15:9).

We get better acquainted with Jesus as he reveals more about himself by his words, attitudes, and actions. He bids us "come to me" and "learn from me" and "follow me," and then we will be better prepared to fulfill the mission to which he is calling us in the third millennium.

Growing in Hope by the Holy Spirit. The second phase of the renewal, in the year 1998, "will be dedicated in a particular way to the Holy Spirit and to his sanctifying presence within the community of Christ's disciples."[2] The Holy Father stated in his apostolic letter:

> Mary, who conceived the Incarnate Word by the power of the Holy Spirit and then in the whole of her life allowed herself to be guided by his interior activity will be contemplated and imitated during this year above all as the woman who was docile to the voice of the Spirit....[3]

Mary's docility to the inspirations and guidance of the Holy Spirit will lead us to an "appreciation of the presence and activity of the Spirit" within us.[4] Her fervent hope makes her a radiant model for us in these days of the Great Renewal.

Growing in Love for the Father. The third phase, in the year 1999, will be our "pilgrimage to the house of the Father." In making our commitment to the Father, "Mary Most Holy, the highly favored daughter of the Father, will appear before the eyes of believers as the perfect model of love towards both God and neighbor."[5] During this time we will contemplate the unconditional love of the Father for us and for every human creature.

When we review the primary objectives of the millennial renewal, our first reaction may be a feeling of inadequacy to carry out such a demanding program. And yet the "success" of this endeavor depends upon how wholeheartedly we and all other Christians respond to the challenge. In all three stages of the millennial renewal, Mary is present and leads us in our endeavors to deepen our relationship with the Lord.

The Lord never asks us to do anything without his help and support. "Apart from me you can do nothing," our Lord cautions us (Jn 15:5). Yet this caution also contains a promise: *with* him we can do *all things.* From the cross he gave us his own Mother as our model and exemplar. In the pages that follow, we will discover how she assists us with her maternal guidance and her powerful support.

How This Book Is Structured

In this volume we present two different aspects of Mary's maternal mission.

Part One. In the first section, chapters 1 to 6, we recall the four better-known apparitions of Mary and single out the principal request made during each appearance:

- At Guadalupe (1531), Our Lady enkindled a fervent faith in the hearts of the native Aztec people, which led them to Jesus and the Christian way of life.

- At Lourdes (1858), Mary spoke of the necessity of healing and holiness, and announced that she is the Immaculate Conception.

- At Fatima (1917), Mary asked us to imitate her lifestyle by consecrating ourselves to her Immaculate Heart, urging us to pray and live the rosary devotion.

- At Medjugorje (since 1981), Mary continues to refocus our attention on the sacramental life of the Church. In the sacraments we meet the Person of Jesus so that he can share his divine life and love with us.

In all her messages, Mary invites us to develop a dynamic faith, fervent prayer, sincere reconciliation, and total acquiescence to God's will.

Part Two. In chapters 7 to 12, we reflect on Mary's life, how perfectly she lived the gospel way of life proclaimed by Jesus. As we reflect on some of the virtues which characterize Mary, we find her an ideal model for our daily living.

Contemplating Mary as a woman who was docile and obedient to the Holy Spirit, we will become more attentive to the Spirit's promptings in our own lives. Mary's life of prayer will inspire us to pray more fervently and profoundly. Following our Mother as the light in the faith crisis in our world, our own faith and hope will become more dynamic and operative—even through periods of intense suffering. Recalling Mary's role as the first and perfect disciple of Jesus, we will naturally resolve to recommit ourselves to follow our Lord with greater zeal and enthusiasm, entrusting ourselves to Mary's motherly intercession as we do so.

How to Use This Book

Mary, Star of the New Millennium, is not a book to be read rapidly. The thoughts on these pages should lead us to a gradual appreciation of Mary, and of our Mother's deep concern for a Great Renewal in the Church and in the world. Each chapter is intended to give us an insight into the beauty of Mary's soul with the hope that we may be inspired and motivated to emulate her example. As the Star leading us to Jesus, Mary is eagerly waiting to accompany us on our journey.

Read reflectively and prayerfully, one chapter at a time. Select a thought, an expression, or insight from it upon which to meditate. Rest quietly, even wordlessly, with the Lord as a thought or word finds a home in your heart. As you do this, you will be drawn to review your own life to ascertain if your heart and will are in tune with the Lord's, as Mary's were.

As we consider Mary's perfect model of discipleship, we can be certain that the Lord will be molding and transforming us into dedicated disciples as we strive to become more like his Mother. Hand in hand with our Mother Mary, let us continue our journey into the Great Renewal of the third millennium.

A Personal Reflection

For personal reasons I was happy to prepare these reflections on Mary's special role as the Star guiding us into the third millennium. When I was twelve years old, the Lord called my own mother to her heavenly reward. On her deathbed she consoled me with the promise that now I would have two mothers in heaven to watch over me and pray for me, herself and the Mother of Jesus. As a loving mother, she advised me to come to both of them in prayer before I made any important decision in my life.

Throughout the years I have tried to follow my mother's advice. I have found that both of my mothers were true to their promise. This manuscript was prepared to say, *Thank you, God,* for my two mothers, and to thank you, Mothers, for being the greatest mothers anyone could have.

PART I

MESSAGES FROM MARY TO THE MODERN-DAY CHURCH

In this section we recall Mary's appearances throughout history as she reveals her loving concern for us and prepares the groundwork for our entry into the Great Jubilee of the third millennium.

ONE

MARY, GUIDING STAR OF THE NEW MILLENNIUM

"We have seen his star in the East."
MATTHEW 2:2

"Lead, kindly light."
JOHN HENRY NEWMAN

During the latter part of this second millennium, God has been preparing us for the great revitalization of the Christian way of life, a renewal we are eagerly anticipating to take place in the third millennium. In order to recognize and appreciate the plan which God is initiating in our society, we must briefly survey the course of salvation history up to the present time.

Given our broken human nature, so prone to sin, we can easily drift from the way of life the Lord set before us. In the midst of the noise, speed, and confusion of our age, we are apt to take a wrong off-ramp as we journey down the highway of life. We then find ourselves lost in a maze of conflicting trends and lifestyles, which causes us to drift more and more away from the Lord. Even though Jesus says: "I am standing at the door knocking" (Rv 3:20), we may not hear him in the depths of our being.

Wandering in the dense mist of our own making, we may lose

sight of God and become uncertain, skeptical, fearful. Faith weakens, and gives rise to doubts and indifference. We become deaf to the gentle promptings of the Holy Spirit, and lose our sense of direction. Under these conditions, peace, serenity, and genuine joy vanish from our hearts. Francis Thompson masterfully captures the anguish of those determined to remain lost, in his celebrated poem, "The Hound of Heaven":

> I fled Him down, down the nights and down the days;
>   I fled Him, down the arches of the years;
> I fled Him down the labyrinthine ways
>   of my own mind, and in the midst of tears,
> I hid from Him.... [1]

These poetic reflections certainly apply to our society today, but there still remains great hope, since the Hound of Heaven never gives up on us. Because of his unconditional and immutable love, our gracious God never gives up on us, nor will he ever abandon us. Many times he has gone to great lengths to arrest our attention and to rivet our focus on our privileged vocation as his disciples.

A Look at History

When God chose the Israelites of the Old Testament times, he revealed to them that he alone was the only true God, and he formed a covenant with them: "So shall you be my people, and I will be your God" (Jer 11:4).

The long history of faith of the Hebrew people began when the Lord led Abraham into the land of Canaan. God promised Abraham that he would become a great nation if he remained faithful to God (see Gen 12:2). As long as Abraham and his descendants honored this covenant, they enjoyed a deep and lasting relationship with God, who blessed them with peace and prosperity.

However, the time came when the Hebrew people no longer observed this covenant as Abraham had. In Genesis chapters 42-47 we read that crops began to fail, and when famine was imminent, Jacob sent his sons to Egypt for food. This was the beginning of the migration of the Chosen People into the land of Egypt, where the inhabitants worshiped pagan deities and knew nothing of the one true God. Gradually the Israelites were influenced by their pagan neighbors and began to participate in the worship of false gods and to drift away from the worship of the God of Abraham, Isaac, and Jacob. As they drew further and further away from God, the Israelites lost the protection of the covenant, and became enslaved by the Egyptians. This continued until the time of Moses, whom God sent to free them from the bonds of slavery.

After the Lord freed them from the slavery of Egypt, he led them into the desert. There they enkindled their faith and trust in him, and he transformed them into a people after his own mind and heart. Through Moses on Mount Sinai, he gave them the Ten Commandments, a code of morality as the norm for their daily living. He promised them that if they were faithful, he would protect and provide for them at all times. They, in turn, pledged their loyalty and committed themselves to live according to his law.

As time went on, the Chosen People were intrigued by the pagan cults and false gods of their neighbors. Gradually they drifted away from the Lord and abandoned their pledged allegiance to serve only the one true God.

In spite of their infidelities, God did not reject or abandon them. At various periods in their history, he sent prophets to warn them of their apostasy and to urge them to return to the worship of the one true God. They turned a deaf ear in response: the prophets were ridiculed, persecuted, and even killed. As a last resort, God permitted the Israelites to be dragged off into captivity. Their temple was destroyed, and countless numbers were slain by their enemies.

At other times, the Chosen People did listen to the exhortations of the prophets. They acknowledged their sinfulness, repented, sought forgiveness, and dedicated themselves once again to the Lord, and they were spared by a compassionate, merciful God.

The Church in the World Today

In many ways our actions reflect the infidelities of the Chosen People. Like the Israelites, we are drifting away from God and the Christian way of life to which we have been called. God's moral code is often ignored; his Law is considered "outdated." In the minds of many, worship has become optional and the sacramental life of the Church irrelevant.

But God calls out to us, as he called out to the people of Israel. Down through the centuries, Mary has fulfilled a special prophetic role similar to that of the seers in the Old Testament. At various times the Lord sends Mary to appear on earth to alert, caution, and warn the people of God of some insidious dangers threatening our relationship with him and weaning us away from his way of life. If these attacks have already made inroads in our life or weakened our dedication to the Lord, Mary encourages us to repent and recommit ourselves to the Lord who assured us, "I am the way, and the truth, and the life" (Jn 14:6).

Many people have disregarded Mary's prophetic voice. But in his grace, God has sent another voice to reinforce her message and counteract the growing attitude of indifference—to lead us back to the Source of our life. It is the voice of our Holy Father.

The Prophetic Voice of Pope John Paul II

On numerous occasions Pope John Paul II has issued a clarion call, urging us to prepare for the great reawakening in the coming millennium so that we may fulfill the mission to which the Lord is calling us. He has cautioned us about the intrigues of the evil spirit in our times, and encouraged us to commit ourselves more fully to the Christian way of life laid down in the gospel.

The numerous publications of Pope John Paul II reinforce that call, encouraging us to live a dynamic gospel spirituality. The Holy Father also cautions us that it may not always be easy, but a sure way to victory—our salvation. He writes:

I have felt that the heart of the Gospel is contained in these words. "The Gospel is not a promise of easy success." It does not promise a comfortable life to anyone. It makes demands, and, at the same time, it is a great promise—the promise of eternal life for man, who is subject to the law of death, and the promise of victory through faith for man, who is subject to many trials and setbacks.[2]

The anticipation of the third millennium has enkindled within us an eager and expectant hope for extraordinary things to come in our society. It is a special privilege to live in this era of Christian renewal and revitalization, of reconciliation and conversion.

The reawakening we have already experienced, and will continue to experience even more fully, was initiated by the Second Vatican Council. In his apostolic letter "The Coming of the Third Millennium" Pope John Paul II wrote: "The Second Vatican Council was a providential event, whereby the Church began the more immediate preparation for the Jubilee of the Second Millennium."[3] This council emphasized the importance of nurturing a personal relationship with the Lord, a relationship motivated by love rather than by obligation.

The Marian Year (1986-87) was also an ideal preparation for the coming age. In the same apostolic letter, the Holy Father says: "The Marian Year was as it were an anticipation of the Jubilee, and contained much of what will find fuller expression in the Year 2000."[4]

Pope John Paul II also sets forth the primary objective for which we should strive in this era of renewal: "the strengthening of faith and of the witness of Christians."[5]

A Plan for Renewal

In "The Coming of the Third Millennium" the Holy Father outlines a program which will enable us to fulfill our personal role in the anticipated renewal:

> Everything ought to focus on the primary objective of the Jubilee: the strengthening of faith and of the witness of Christians. It is therefore necessary to inspire in all the faithful a true longing for holiness, a deep desire for conversion and personal renewal in a context of ever more intense prayer and of solidarity with one's neighbor, especially the most needy.[6]

Interestingly, these "keys" to renewal were predominant themes in Mary's appearances at Guadalupe, Fatima, Lourdes, and Medjugorje.

Medjugorje: A strengthening of faith. Threaded throughout all her appearances, Mary's message calling us to holiness, conversion, and renewal begins with a "strengthening of faith." A vibrant faith of commitment and expectancy is imperative for us to grow in holiness and also give witness to others by our lifestyle.

Jesus said plainly: "Apart from me you can do nothing" (Jn 15:5). In her ongoing appearances at Medjugorje, Mary reminds us that there is an overflowing abundance of divine help in the sacramental life of the Church as instituted by Jesus, especially in the Sacrament of Reconciliation and the Eucharistic Celebration.

Lourdes: A true longing for holiness. Mary's primary message at Lourdes was a call to holiness. We become holy by striving to accept and fulfill the will of God in all the happenings of the day. As we contemplate the Person of Jesus as a gracious, loving, caring God, we will become more like him, putting on his mind and heart.

Fatima: Personal renewal in the context of ever more intense prayer. Mary's message at Fatima called the faithful to intense prayer. We are not necessarily called to spend more time in prayer, nor to add additional prayers to our regular list of petitions, sorrow, thanksgiving, and praise. Rather we are to strive to pray ever more intensely as we move from vocal prayer into meditation and on into contemplation.

Guadalupe: Solidarity with one's neighbor, especially the most needy. As we shall read later, Our Lady of Guadalupe came not to the wealthy and influential, but to the poor who needed to hear her message. In the same way, Jesus commands us to love our neighbor as ourselves. Only when we listen with our heart to the Lord telling us how much he loves us and how precious we are to him, only then can we reach out in love to all those the Lord permits to come into our life.

We should always be willing to lend a helping hand to anyone in need, but we must also be alert to all those who are spiritually needy—by praying for them, sharing our faith with them, and striving to lead them to Jesus by our words, attitudes, and actions.

The Gift of Mary's Presence Among Us

That we might be better equipped to fulfill the role to which the Lord is calling us in these days of the millennial renewal, the Holy Spirit has bestowed on us special charisms. A charism is a gift or grace of the Holy Spirit conferred on us primarily to be used for the upbuilding of the Church, for the good of others, and for the needs of the world (see Rom 12:6, 1 Cor 12:4). As committed Christians, we are enriched with a variety of charisms to fulfill our apostolic mission in life. These special gifts of the Holy Spirit are evident in the lives of devoted parents, dedicated teachers, the whole host of volunteers who are vitally concerned about the spiritual and temporal welfare of others. In fact, these charisms are quite obvious in the lives of all Christians who are striving to walk in the way of the Lord.

In addition to these graces, we have been given another extraordinary gift: Mary's spiritual presence with us, her shining example, and her powerful intercession. From the cross, Jesus gave us Mary's presence when he said to John, the beloved disciple, "Behold, your Mother" (Jn 19:27). Scripture scholars maintain that the word "disciple" is a collective noun including all those seeking salvation. For that reason, the Church has understood and taught for two thousand years that Jesus was giving Mary not only to John, but to us as well.

Mary paves the way for us through her example and guides us on our journey. She also picks us up when we falter and fall in our efforts to revitalize our own spiritual lives and to bring others to a deeper appreciation of the Great Renewal in which we are involved.

Mary's whole life was a manifestation of the special charisms with which she was endowed. As we contemplate Mary's presence with Elizabeth, our prayer life develops; Mary's presence on Calvary encourages us in time of trial; her presence in the Upper Room on the first Pentecost keeps us open and receptive to the transforming power of the Holy Spirit. We will discuss these episodes more fully in the second half of this book.

As we prayerfully reflect on Mary's way of life, we will recognize, nurture, and manifest our own God-given charisms. This in turn enables us to undertake the various steps on the road to renewal. The gifts and graces of the Holy Spirit will inspire, lead, and sustain us as we enter more deeply into the Great Renewal of the third millennium. We can be certain that the charism of Mary's presence with us is just as powerful as it was on the day of the first Pentecost.

Are We Ready for Renewal?

We have nothing to fear from the change God wishes to work in us as a result of this revitalization. The blessings and fruits of renewal will not descend suddenly on our society like a mighty crusade. It will not happen overnight, nor will it happen against our will. God does not force himself upon us, but patiently waits for us to be receptive and cooperative to his inspirations and guidance in these days of renewal.

During his ministry on earth, Jesus was always pleased when people responded to him and his teachings with simple, humble faith. On one occasion while teaching and healing he paused to pray: "I thank thee, Father, Lord of heaven and earth, that thou hast hidden these things from the wise and understanding and revealed them to babes" (Mt 11:25). By contrast, Matthew tells us that Jesus was unable to minister to the people of Nazareth who rejected Jesus. Matthew tells us: "He did not do many mighty works there, because of their unbelief" (Mt 13:58). A humble, trusting openness to the Lord is fertile soil in which a genuine Christlike disposition is nurtured, matures, and flourishes.

Consider for a moment the various visionaries to whom Mary has appeared. Their personal qualities give us an insight into the spiritual qualities our heavenly Father wants us to develop, that he may work in us and through us.

The persons to whom Mary has appeared have been, for the most part, young, innocent people with a simple, trusting faith. In Israel these people would be classified as *anawim,* or the quiet people. These were humble, simple, prayerful people who were looking for the coming of the Messiah. Simeon and Anna were regarded as *anawim* (see Lk 2:25ff).

Mary seems to seek out the simple and quiet people in our day and age as well. At Guadalupe, Our Lady appeared to Juan Diego, a pious peasant convert of simple faith, as he was on his way to Mass one morning. Bernadette was an uneducated shepherdess at Lourdes. Her testimony was considered trustworthy *because* she did not know what Our Lady meant when she said: "I am the Immaculate Conception." The three children at Fatima were encouraged by Our Lady to learn to read, and probably learned the prayers of the Rosary at home. The original six children of Medjugorje were also humble, innocent children with a simple faith and trust in God.

We have much to learn from these modern-day *anawim.* A humble disposition of heart and mind keeps us more readily attuned to the inspirations of the Holy Spirit. It is the faith, zeal, and commitment of every Christian that will enable us to transform our society with the love and life of Christ. As every person of goodwill strives to live a Christlike way of life as perfectly as

Mary did, the great blessings of the renewal will gradually influence our world.

St. Paul encourages those who may doubt the extent of their influence in renewing society: "Do not be overcome by evil, but overcome evil with good" (Rom 12:21). This advice was rephrased by Father James Keller, founder of the Christophers, in the movement's well-known slogan: "Better to light one candle than to curse the darkness." If we pass the light of our candle to others, our own light will not be extinguished or diminished, but will be multiplied and reflected far and wide.

With Mary's lifestyle as our model and her maternal guidance and powerful prayer as our support, we launch out to discover our special role. May we be tireless in our efforts to fulfill the mission to which the Lord is calling us in these precious days of the millennial renewal.

TWO

GUADALUPE:
A CALL TO BUILD A
COMMUNITY OF FAITH

"This is the victory that conquers the world, our faith."
1 JOHN 5:4

*"Everything ought to focus on the primary
objective of the jubilee: the strengthening
of faith and of the witness of Christians."*
POPE JOHN PAUL II

When the New World was discovered, it was to be, according to the divine plan, a world deeply imbued with a strong Christian faith. God permitted extraordinary events to take place at Guadalupe in order to lead the natives as well as the settlers into forming a community of faith.

It all began on a cold December day in 1531, as the Spanish explorers and missionaries were settling in that part of the western hemisphere now known as Mexico. Millions of Aztec Indians had migrated from South America and settled in this region. They were a strong, proud people. For generations they worshiped pagan celestial deities—the sun, stars, and a moon-shaped stone god. To appease their gods, and to ensure happiness and avert calamities, they even offered human sacrifices to these pagan deities.

When the Spanish conquistadors arrived, they tried to force the Aztecs to abandon their pagan worship and become Christians. Their misguided zeal was tarnished by their greed as they enslaved the natives, stole their treasures, and destroyed their temples. The Franciscan missionaries who came with the conquistadors did not condone the destruction and robbery of the pagan temples. However, because the Franciscans were also Spanish, the Aztec people did not trust their well-meaning efforts. Conversions were very few.

Tepeyac Hill

On December 9, 1531, an extraordinary phenomenon brought about a change in the receptivity of the Aztecs that exceeded any human expectations. Mary, the Mother of Jesus, appeared to Juan Diego, a poor Aztec convert on Tepeyac Hill as he was on his way to Mass. Mary identifies herself only as the messenger of the true God:

> Dear little son, I love you. I want you to know who I am. I am the ever-virgin Mary, Mother of the true God, the God who gives life and maintains it in existence. He created all things. He is in all places. He is Lord of heaven and earth. I desire a temple or church at this place where I will show my compassion to your people and to all who sincerely ask my help in their work and in their sorrows. Here, I will see their tears; I will console them and they will be at ease. So run to Mexico City and tell the Lord Bishop all that you have seen and heard.

It was no easy matter to see the bishop. Juan was a simple soul, and he had no appointment. The servants of the bishop kept him waiting and tried to dissuade him. They treated him roughly, and let him wait in a corner for a long time. Finally he found himself in the presence of the bishop.

The bishop was courteous and kind, but the story of that encounter and Juan's dialogue with the Lady and her desire to build a church in an uninhabited place was a little too much for him to believe. The bishop ended the interview by telling Juan that he could come back any time if he cared to and they would talk further about it.

Each time Juan returned to renew the request that a chapel be built, the bishop listened attentively, but somewhat skeptically. While he was inclined to believe Juan's account, he remained judiciously hesitant and asked for some sign from Our Lady.

Mary graciously obliged. On a cold wintry day, she instructed Juan to climb to the top of the barren Tepeyac Hill to pick the beautiful Castilian roses he would find there. Mary herself arranged the roses in his *tilma,* or poncho, and sent him off to bring them to the bishop.

When Juan opened his *tilma,* the roses fell to the floor. The bishop and his staff fell to their knees, overcome with awe and wonder, for the image of Our Lady was miraculously imprinted on the inside of the *tilma.* It is the only portrait we have from heaven of the Mother of God, who is now revered as Our Lady of Guadalupe.

Nor was this the end of the miraculous event. The *tilma* Juan wore has been miraculously preserved without any sign of deterioration for more than four hundred years, in spite of the fact that it has been touched and kissed by thousands of devotees. This fact speaks of the authenticity of this divine event.

In 1921, when persecution of the Church was rampant in Mexico, a bomb exploded beneath the *tilma* with tremendous force. The bomb was planted in a basket of flowers below the sacred image. Its force broke windows in the Basilica, shattered the marble altar, and twisted the bronze crucifix.

But the image of Our Lady—and the glass which covered it—was not damaged.

What Does This Encounter Say to Us?

Mary's appearances since her Assumption, as her life on earth, are a bright light guiding us in our present-day crisis in faith. On these occasions the Lord permits his Mother to appear in order to plead with us to nurture and strengthen the gifts of faith we have received. At Guadalupe, Mary's appearances were instrumental in forming a remarkable community of faith among the Aztecs.

Our benevolent Father always meets us where we are, and accommodates himself to our human understanding and capabilities. This is evident in Our Lady's appearances at Guadalupe. There, everything about Mary's physical appearance was highly significant to the Aztec people. Her features were that of a beautiful young Aztec woman. Her posture and attire had deep religious meaning in Aztec culture: Mary stood in front of the sun, a sign to the Aztec that her power was greater than that of the sun god. She stood on the crescent moon to manifest her power over their stone moon god. As a messenger she was empowered by God, yet her hands were folded in prayer; her posture was one of humility and of worship of the One greater than she.

Mary's distinctive apparel and all the signs about her indicated to the Aztecs that she was sent by the one true God. The Aztecs understood that she was only a messenger: she was carried by two angels, which are pictured in the *tilma* at her feet. (The Aztecs believed that gods come on their own power, and so they understood that she herself was not a god.)

These and many other significant features enkindled faith in Aztec hearts and stirred belief in the authenticity of these divine events. Because of Mary's visitation, the Aztecs were receptive to the catechesis of the missionaries, who told them of the Blessed Trinity. The Aztecs were also pleased when Our Lady asked for a temple to be erected beyond the territory controlled by the Spanish. This temple was to replace the temple on Tepeyac Hill to the Aztecs' Mother-goddess, a snake-woman to whom human sacrifice—usually female—was offered.

Historians maintain that within seven years after the apparitions, some eight million Aztec people received the gift of faith, were baptized, and formed a strong, dynamic Christian community. Their faith not only survived but increased greatly throughout the centuries.

Called to Community

Our Lady's message at Guadalupe is timely for us. In this period of the millennial renewal we are asked to build a vibrant Christian community based on loving concern for others.

One of the objectives of the renewal is "to inspire in all the faithful a solidarity with one's neighbor, especially the most needy."[1] The "most needy" includes not only the materially poor but all those who have great spiritual needs, since they have little or no knowledge of the Lord and his unbounded love for them.

By our Baptism we were incorporated into a privileged community of faith. The Father adopted us as his sons and daughters, and we became special temples of the Holy Spirit. As members of the family of God we are in reality brothers and sisters to each other.

We are destined for community "because God's love has been poured into our hearts through the Holy Spirit who has been given to us" (Rom 5:5). Genuine Christian community is founded not on rules and regulations, but on love for one another. In the Eucharistic prayers at Mass, we pray for this unity:

> May all of us who share in the body and blood of Christ be brought together in unity by the Holy Spirit.
> EUCHARISTIC PRAYER II

> Grant that we, who are nourished by his body and blood, may be filled with his Holy Spirit and become one body, one spirit in Christ.
> EUCHARISTIC PRAYER III

So, how are we to begin? Here are a few guidelines to assist us in our endeavors.

Community begins on a small scale. The family is a good example of a community. It begins with just two people, a husband and a wife. Eventually the community "expands" to include children, and as the family grows, its influence extends outside the home. In the same way, Christian community begins small, and as it grows, through outreach and prayer, its influence is felt outside the borders of the immediate group.

Quiet times together are important. It is necessary to spend relaxed time with one another, showing real concern for each other. This is important to do both when times are good and when they are hard.

Gratitude is an important ingredient in community-building. Frequent expressions of gratitude and appreciation, as well as expressions of affection and respect, help a group of people to grow closer together and make the community stronger.

Prayer is a powerful part of any community. Prayer is the most powerful unifying force in building an authentic community. No other means can knit minds and hearts in close mutual understanding and effort. Jesus assures us: "Where two or three are gathered in my name, there am I in the midst of them" (Mt 18:20).

In recent years the Church has endeavored to bring us to a deeper sense and appreciation of the Mass as a praying community. To accomplish this, the Church has arranged for greater participation in the liturgy through deacons, lectors, acolytes, and community singing and praying. Jesus reminds of the great power of communal prayer when he says: "Again I say to you, if two of you agree on earth about anything they ask, it will be done for them by my Father" (Mt 18:19). On another occasion he said: "Truly, truly, I say to you, if you ask anything of the Father, he will give it to you in my name" (Jn 16:23).

The Praying Heart of Mary

Like every good mother, Mary is at the heart of her family. The contemplative nature of Mary's prayer life is characterized by a passage in the Gospel of Luke, in which Mary and Joseph discover Jesus in the temple: "His mother kept all these things in her heart" (Lk 2:51). Throughout her earthly life, her heart pondered the ways of God as she saw him work in her life and in the lives of her family. This is the essence of contemplative prayer.

Her example continues to guide us. Just as Mary was present in the Upper Room as the Church was being born, she is also present in the Church today. She implores, pleads, and promises her help to weld all the members of the Body of Christ into a dynamic Christian community of faith, just as she did at Guadalupe. She is rightly titled "Mother of the Church."

With Our Lady as "the Star which safely guides our steps to the Lord," may the days of the Great Jubilee mold and transform us into a vibrant, dynamic, operative community of expectant faith in which the Lord will reign supreme. Then we will be blessed with the love, peace, and joy which only the Lord can give, and we will be on our way to the Great Renewal.

THREE

LOURDES:
A CALL TO HEALING
AND HOLINESS

"For he who is mighty has done great things for me."
LUKE 1:49

*"It is therefore necessary to inspire in all the
faithful a true longing for holiness."*
POPE JOHN PAUL II

History is forever repeating itself, says the old adage. Human nature, with its propensity to pride and self-gratification, often prompts us to lose focus on the way of life to which the Lord has called us.

In today's society this tendency can be seen in the errors that creep up under the label of relativism. These errors incline many people to follow the standards set up by hedonistic society. Some of these people, seeking to be accepted in the world, are inclined to live according to society's view of what is morally right and wrong. Others maintain that everyone has a right to decide for themselves what is right and wrong, and so they disregard the code of ethics the Lord has given us.

This is not the first time in history that a false philosophy has arisen to dull Christians' sense of sin and wean them away from their commitment as followers of the Lord.

In the eighteenth and nineteenth centuries, several false and heretical philosophies sprang up and began to make vast inroads into European culture, especially in France. The religious atmosphere of the time was becoming more empirical, maintaining that the only real truth is that which can be learned through experience. These atheistic, rationalistic tenets left no place for God or the supernatural. As a result, people gradually came to believe that there was no such thing as sin, for if God did not exist, there was no place for a moral code. As more and more people turned away from God, they formed their own code of ethics, and lived by their own standards of morality. This resulted in all kinds of injustices, human rights violations, and a host of other evils.

In this and in similar crises, God sent Mary to caution and warn us of these insidious ploys of the Evil One, and to encourage us to return to the way of the Lord. In 1858 at Lourdes, France, Our Lady was plunged into the midst of this social climate to warn people of this demonic influence and to plead for conversion. She urged them to seek healing of mind and heart and to recommit themselves to God and to the way of life he mapped out for his people.

To counter the dangerous influence of the heretical philosophies of the day, Our Lady appeared to Bernadette Soubirous eighteen times between February 11 and July 16, 1858. During the March appearance, she gave Bernadette a specific commission: "Go tell the priests to have a chapel built here and come here in procession." That original chapel has been replaced many times to accommodate larger groups of devotees. At the present time it has developed into a major basilica known as the Rosary Basilica. Millions of people come each year to honor Mary, to thank the Lord for his Mother, and to implore her powerful intercession for a vast variety of blessings and healings of body, soul, and spirit.

This side of heaven, no one will ever know the number of

miracles of grace that have been wrought at Lourdes. Countless numbers of people have received the gift of faith or had their faith greatly strengthened here. Many times the skeptic who came to scoff remained to pray.

"I Am the Immaculate Conception"

It was not until her last appearance at Lourdes that Our Lady revealed her identity: "I am the Immaculate Conception." Bernadette, an unlettered village girl, had passed on Mary's message without realizing what it meant. She was not aware that in 1854 Pope Pius IX had declared as official Church teaching the truth that Mary was immaculately conceived, with no stain of original sin.[1]

Mary's declaration is both the message and the challenge of Lourdes. While we can never claim immunity from original sin, Our Lady's unique privilege challenges us to avoid sin as much as possible in our lives. A true longing for holiness is the gift Mary wishes to instill within us.

Down through the years Lourdes sends forth an unmistakable call for greater holiness of life. This holiness is a quality of striving to keep our minds and hearts in tune with the Lord and having an ever ready "yes" to his will, as Mary did throughout her whole life on earth.

When God sent his Mother to appear at Lourdes, he gave us an incomparable model of acquiescence to the Lord's divine will. Throughout Mary's life she never reneged on the commitment she made at the time of the Annunciation: "Behold, I am the handmaid of the Lord; let it be to me according to your word" (Lk 1:38).

"Do Whatever He Tells You"

Our Lady's solemn declaration "I am the Immaculate Conception" serves to inspire and motivate all those who love her to strive for greater personal perfection. Its challenge to holiness counteracts the insidious influences of relativism by its emphasis on obeying first the laws of God.

Mary's program to attain genuine holiness is quite brief and is intended for implementation throughout our entire sojourn on earth:

Do whatever he tells you.   JOHN 2:5

How simple her maternal directive—only five words—but how difficult to carry out in our daily living! Sheer willpower alone will never suffice here.

In Mary's life, however, we discover the secret of progress in holiness and the essential element in her motivation. Mary faithfully fulfilled God's will for her because of her intense love. Our motivation, likewise, must be based on love. If we love someone, we are willing to do anything within our power to please that person. Nothing seems too hard. As a Bantu proverb puts it, "Love makes a burden light as a cloud."

"If you love me, you will keep my commandments," Jesus says (Jn 14:15). For those who love God it is no burden to obey him. Keeping his commandments may not always be easy, but love makes it possible to take on even the hardest challenges. Mary shows us how to do this wholeheartedly, with peace and joy.

A Haven of Healing

The countless healings of mind, body, and soul that have taken place at Lourdes since 1858 are a powerful testimony to Mary's loving concern for the suffering, and of her active intercession in the healing process.

All of us, whether sick in body or not, need certain healings. As we try to lead a more perfect life, it is important that we come to see this. To walk more closely in the Lord's footsteps, we must be healed of our wavering faith, our pride, our self-centeredness, our lack of love for certain people, our reluctance to enter into ever more intense prayer.

As we strive more earnestly to grow in holiness, we are not always aware of this healing or conversion taking place within. At times we may experience a change of attitude taking place as we enjoy greater peace and tranquility of mind and heart. This interior spiritual healing also brings with it physical and psychological healings, as worries and anxieties seem to evaporate. Often our physical well-being improves, as do our mental attitudes.

During his sojourn on earth, Jesus was often surrounded by scores of people who came to him for healing: the blind and deaf, the sick and lame. As we search the Scriptures, we realize that Jesus always healed the whole person. As he restored broken bodies, he also forgave people's sins and filled them with peace.

Through Mary's intercession, Jesus continues his healing mission today. Scriptures tell us "Jesus Christ is the same yesterday, today, and for ever" (Heb 13:8). He heals through the sacramental life he instituted in the Church, and he also continues to bless us with his healing presence in the sacraments. The Lord's ongoing healing mission is especially evident in the Sacrament of the Anointing of the Sick. In this Sacrament, Jesus heals spiritually by bringing his peace, patience, and joy with the assurance of his love, mercy, and compassion. He also heals physically by speeding a person's recovery if this is in God's plan for the spiritual and temporal welfare of the person.

Watch Out for Pitfalls!

As we learn to appreciate more fully Mary's loving, maternal concern, our love and devotion for our Mother will increase. And because we tend to emulate those we love, we will be motivated to strive more earnestly to imitate her holiness. In our resolve to make greater efforts toward a holier way of life, we must recognize and renounce current moral standards that could creep in and weaken our resolve to do what is right.

The trap of relativism. As mentioned earlier, many people around us—concerned with being accepted by their peers—have allowed society to dictate their moral standards. In this permissive climate we too may begin to view God's standards as too restrictive. Gradually our commitment to the moral code Jesus set forth may weaken; we may become indifferent to the truth and may even start rationalizing away our wrongdoing.

The best way to combat this relativism is to stay on guard against the subtle influences that may creep into our thinking. An effective way to do this is to steep our minds in Scripture. This is the practical advice which the psalmist offers us in our struggle to avoid sin and grow in holiness:

Happy are those who do not follow the advice of the wicked, or take the path that sinners tread, or sit in the seat of scoffers; but delight in the law of the Lord, and on his law they meditate day and night.   PSALMS 1:1-2, NRSV

This psalm is sometimes called a prayer for discernment, since it cautions us to avoid the company of those persons who would lead us away from the Lord. It also encourages us to keep our focus on the Lord and "delight in the law of the Lord." By listening prayerfully, at the core of our being, to the Lord's Word in Scripture, we come to know him with a heart-knowledge that enkindles our own love for him.

The sacraments, too, are filled with the divine power to assist us to walk in his way as we journey though life. The Sacrament of Reconciliation is not only a rite in which we receive forgiveness and pardon; it also heals the wayward tendencies and weaknesses within us. Jesus is eager to come to us in the Eucharist to keep us aware of his boundless love for us and to fill us with the strength and courage to meet the challenges of each day. The Eucharist is also a privileged opportunity for us to offer ourselves with all that we are and do to the Lord, who sanctifies our gift and presents it to the Father in our name.

The comparison trap. Another subtle, insidious influence in our thinking is a prideful tendency to compare ourselves to others. This may happen as we read about scandals in the newspaper or pass the local newsstand with its trash tabloids mirroring the exploits of so-called celebrities. "What degrading escapades!" we may tell ourselves. "I would never do something like *that!*" Far better—and more accurate—for us to remember on those occasions that "there, but for the grace of God, go I!"

How can we avoid the smug superiority which blinds us to our own waywardness and infidelities? The Holy Spirit will help us here, if we have the courage and honesty to ask him to point out our sins and failings. As he does, we may be surprised to have our attention drawn to things we may not have considered very serious. A brief survey of our life can also be a helpful aid to progress in holiness. For example, we might ask ourselves:

- Am I really trying to love those around me? Even the ones who are difficult to love?

- Am I generous with my resources? Or do I go my own way without reaching out to others?

- Do I consistently thank the Lord for his bounteous blessings? Or do I complain about the things I don't have?

- Do I readily recognize the will of God in all the happenings of the day?

Such an inventory will keep us humble, which is a major step on the road to perfection.

Let It Begin in Me

Many years have intervened since Our Lady announced her message at Lourdes, inviting us to strive for greater holiness. Father Leo Boyle writes in *The Story of Lourdes*, "The message [Mary] gave to St. Bernadette is one of faith that men may believe in the truth taught by her Divine Son, of hope that they may trust in his promises, of charity that they may love him."[2] Her maternal request reflects the teaching of Jesus in the Gospel of Matthew:

Be perfect, as your heavenly Father is perfect.   MATTHEW 5:48

This instruction is brief, but it embraces a whole way of life. How are we to accomplish this task? How does one work toward holiness in this life?

The Second Vatican Council, which took place from 1963 to

1965, took up Our Lady's refrain at Lourdes. Especially in its "Dogmatic Constitution on the Church" *(Lumen Gentium)*, it urged all of us to avoid sin and strive for greater holiness:

> All the faithful of Christ are invited to strive for holiness and perfection of their own state. Indeed, they have an obligation so to strive.[3]

In the book of Colossians, the apostle Paul outlined some specific details about how to achieve this holiness of life.

> As God's chosen ones, holy and beloved, clothe yourselves with compassion, kindness, humility, meekness and patience. Bear with one another and, if anyone has a complaint against another, forgive each other; just as the Lord has forgiven you, so you must also forgive. Above all clothe yourselves with love, which binds everything together in perfect harmony.
>
> And let the peace of Christ rule in your hearts, to which indeed you were called in one body. And be thankful.
>
> Let the word of Christ dwell in you richly; teach and admonish one another in all wisdom; and with gratitude in your hearts sing psalms, hymns, and spiritual songs to God. And whatever you do, in word or deed, do everything in the name of the Lord Jesus giving thanks to God the Father through him. COLOSSIANS 3:12-17, NRSV

These spiritual guidelines presented by St. Paul to the Colossians were clearly and completely evident in the life of our Blessed Mother throughout her sojourn on earth. At Lourdes she reiterated these guidelines, which have resulted in the countless ongoing spiritual and physical healings that continue to this day.

These same recommendations are highlighted as the primary

objectives of the millennial renewal in the Apostolic Letter of Pope John Paul II, "The Coming of the Third Millennium." They challenge us to a deeper, more personal renewal by a true longing for holiness, a greater capacity for prayer, and a stronger desire for solidarity with our neighbors, especially those who are poor.[4]

As we reflect on key phrases in the Book of Colossians, we can more readily put them into practice in our own lives.

"[We are] God's chosen ones, holy and beloved...." We are God's chosen ones, for the Lord says, "I have called you by name, you are mine" (Is 43:1). What an extraordinary privilege to be chosen and given the gift of faith!

"Compassion, kindness, humility, meekness, and patience...." During his earthly sojourn Jesus himself manifested these virtues to which he calls us. To encourage us, Jesus says, "I have given you a model to follow, so that as I have done for you, you should do also" (Jn 13:15, NRSV).

"Bear with one another and forgive each other...." We will often fail in our efforts to put virtue into practice. Reconciliation and forgiveness is the key to attaining a disposition of grace and forgiveness. Remembering Jesus' prayer from the cross will give us courage: "Father, forgive them; for they know not what they do" (Lk 23:34).

"Let the peace of Christ rule in your hearts...." This is the goal for all Christians. We radiate the peace of Christ when we are reconciled with God, when we accept ourselves as we are and are willing to accept others as they are. The peace in our hearts will be evident to everyone we meet.

"Be thankful...." This is one of the primary duties of every Christian. Think of the lesson Jesus taught us in the account of the ten lepers (see Lk 17:11-19). We can demonstrate our gratitude to God by using well all the gifts, graces, and inspirations he sends our way.

"Let the word of Christ dwell in you richly...." When God's Word finds a home in our hearts, it molds and transforms us into the kind of person the Lord calls us to be.

"Whatever you do, in word or deed...." Doing precisely, to the best of our ability, what the Lord asks of us each day is the safest and surest way on our journey heavenward. It is also the most powerful way of expressing our love for God. Love always desires to do what will please the beloved. How aptly our Mother says: "Do whatever he tells you" (Jn 2:5). Love must be our motivating power. Jesus summarized our whole Christian way of life in the twofold commandment to love God above all things, and to love our neighbor as ourselves (see Mt 22:37-39).

As we seek the grace and guidance of the Holy Spirit, we will be ready for all the Lord has in store for us as the new millennium approaches. As every follower of the Lord resolves to accept the challenge of greater personal holiness, our lives will be renewed and revitalized.

FOUR

Fatima:
A Call to Prayer
and Commitment

*"Commit your way to the Lord;
trust in him, and he will act."*
Psalms 37:5

*"Mary will be contemplated and imitated
above all as the woman who was docile to the
voice of the Spirit, a woman of silence and
attentiveness, a woman of hope."*
Pope John Paul II

E ven a casual acquaintance with the God of the Old Testament
will convince us of the providential, protective love of God
for the Chosen People. Patiently he sent prophets to caution, warn,
and encourage them in pursuing the way of life to which he had
called them. How frequently he came to their rescue in times of
war, how often he freed them when they were led off into captivity.

Since the Lord is eternally the same, yesterday, today, and forever, and since he has called us into this same covenant love relationship, God's loving concern watches over us at all times and in
all situations as well.

Perhaps there is no place where the love of God can be so clearly seen as in a time of war. Consider the circumstances surrounding Our Lady's appearance at Fatima. World War I had been raging in Europe, and other nations were being drawn into the bloody conflict. Leaders of atheistic communism had a firm hold on Russia, and were determined to spread their ideology around the world.

In the midst of this devastation and destruction the Lord sent his Mother to bring hope and reassurance. Her message also offered a plan to end the horrible war, thwart the spread of communism, and eventually hasten the demise of this ideology.

The Story of Fatima

Our Lady appeared at Fatima, Portugal, in 1917 at the Cova da Iria to three shepherd children: Francisco, Jacinta, and Lucia. Standing on a cloud hovering over a small oak tree, Our Lady asked the three young seers to pray the rosary daily and to encourage the spread of the devotion of the Immaculate Heart throughout the world. She promised that if enough people prayed the rosary fervently each day, the war would soon end and eventually Russia would be converted. She appeared six times that year, on the thirteenth day of each month from May to October. Repeatedly Our Lady asked the seers to pray the Rosary and to spread its devotion to others:

"*Say the Rosary every day to earn peace for the world and at the end of the war....*"

"*Say the Rosary, inserting between the mysteries the following ejaculation, 'O My Jesus, forgive us. Save us from the fires of Hell. Bring all souls to Heaven, especially those most in need of Your Mercy....'*"

"I come to ask the consecration of Russia to my Immaculate Heart and the Communion of Reparation on the First Saturdays...."

History has proven the truth of Mary's message and also her powerful intercession with God. Responding to Our Lady's request for a crusade of prayer for the conversion of Russia, we have witnessed the power of prayer by a sudden and peaceful collapse of communism in Eastern Europe. Did not the poet Tennyson say, "More things are wrought by prayer than this world dreams of"?

In October 1930 the devotion to Our Lady of Fatima was authorized under the title of Our Lady of the Rosary. Fatima is among the greatest of the modern Marian shrines.

The Power of the Rosary Revealed in History

When the Christian countries throughout the Mediterranean were threatened by hostile inroads of the Turks, Pope Pius V urged the whole Christian world to intercede with Mary, the Queen of Peace. He called them to pray the rosary, that this threat to their Christian way of life could be averted.

On October 7, 1571 the Christian fleet under the command of Don Juan of Austria defeated the Turks in the naval battle at Lepanto. Each year on October 7, the Church celebrates the Feast of the Rosary to commemorate this tremendous naval victory and to recall Mary's maternal and powerful intercession with the Lord.

Three Levels of Prayer in the Rosary

The rosary is a popular and powerful prayer centering on the Person of Jesus and his redemptive mission, from the announcement of his birth through his suffering, death, and resurrection. It leads us into the three principal methods of prayer. We verbalize the words as our fingers touch each bead (vocal prayer); our thoughts and minds ponder the meaning of the words as well as the mystery upon which we are meditating (meditative prayer); and this moves our hearts into an unspoken oneness in love and appreciation to the Lord (contemplative prayer).

Vocal Prayer. The familiar words of the Creed, the Our Father, the Hail Mary, and the Glory Be provide a foundation for our meditation. Those who find the repetition of these prayers boring or tedious may not have learned to enter into the devotion on a deeper level.

Consider the repetition of prayers of the rosary as a sort of background "music" as we reflect on the scriptural events of each mystery. This is much like what happens when a cyclist pedals along a breathtaking nature trail. He is not aware of the movements of his feet as he pedals along, allowing the beauty of God's creation to fill him with awe and wonder. Similarly, we can allow the words of the rosary to fall from our lips almost effortlessly as our hearts and minds rejoice in the outpouring of God's love revealed in the events of salvation history.

The repetitive nature of these prayers provides another benefit. As the words filter past our consciousness and find a home in our heart, they influence our actions and attitudes, and make us more aware of the Lord's abiding presence. Some psychologists maintain that simply fingering the beads is a form of prayer.

Meditative Prayer. Meditation is a thought process. As we ponder God's events in the christological mysteries of the rosary, our thoughts center on the goodness and love of the Lord, moving us into a spirit of gratitude and praise to such a bounteous God.

The joyful mysteries of the rosary remind us of how lovingly and meticulously the Father planned the coming events of our redemption. Mary's faith, trust, and love of God enabled her to make the total commitment of herself to the Lord. Our own faith is enkindled as we listen to Mary's memorable words: "Let it be to me according to your word" (Lk 1:38). The coming of Jesus, assuming our human nature as a vulnerable, helpless babe, compels us to rejoice as we celebrate his boundless love for us. How eager our heart is to whisper, "I love you, too."

As we walk with Jesus through the sorrowful mysteries, our reflection fills us with a deeper realization of the awful price Jesus paid for our redemption, and the glory that awaits us.

What feelings of joy and triumph we experience as we recall the glorious mysteries of the rosary. The Resurrection of Jesus assures us of our own rising with him and also keeps us aware of his abiding presence with us and within us.

How good to know that Jesus sent the Holy Spirit to enlighten, strengthen, and guide us throughout the labyrinthine maze of our daily living. We rejoice with Mary in her Assumption as she is united with her Divine Son for all eternity. Aware of her powerful intercession, we find peace and reassurance as we pray: "Pray for us sinners now and at the hour of our death." In the rosary we praise, thank, and glorify all three Persons of the Blessed Trinity.

Contemplative Prayer. As we concentrate on the prayers of the rosary we are led into a contemplative prayer posture. This prayer is a wordless prayer, a prayer of listening with the heart. It fills us with an awareness of the Lord's presence, love, power, and concern, enabling us to respond in love to him.

In this prayer posture, we simply rest with the Lord in awe and wonder at the goodness of God. It has a powerful transforming effect on us, conforming us to the mind and heart of the Lord.

In the apostolic letter we are reminded that all the hopes and expectations of the millennium will be realized if we enter into "ever more intense prayer." The rosary is an ideal avenue into deeper, ever more intense prayer.

The Immaculate Heart of Mary

During Our Lady's third apparition at Fatima, on July 13, she requested that devotion and consecration to her Immaculate Heart be spread throughout the world.

When we speak of the heart, we speak of the whole person: his or her personality, character, attitudes, and actions. Likewise, when we speak about Mary as the Immaculate Heart, we are reflecting on her whole lifestyle in committing herself totally to the Lord without any reservation. She made her permanent commitment at the time of the Annunciation: "Behold, I am the handmaid of the Lord; let it be to me according to your word" (Lk 1:38).

The etymology of the world "consecration" informs us that it is derived from two Latin words, *sacer*, "holy," and *con*, meaning "with." Consecration to Mary's Immaculate Heart means to strive "with holiness" with the help and guidance of Mary as our model and exemplar. It means that we have chosen to follow as closely as possible in the footsteps of Mary, our Mother, in fulfilling our mission in life.

When we consecrate ourselves to the Immaculate Heart of Mary, we are promising to live in union with the mind and heart of Mary by following her requests and instructions announced at her many different appearances here on earth.

When we pray the rosary for peace in our own hearts and for peace in the world, we are fulfilling one of Our Lady's requests at Fatima. Imploring God's mercy and forgiveness for sinners and for the conversion of the whole world delights the heart of Mary, the Refuge of Sinners. Striving to do precisely what God asks of us in all the happenings of the day is our attempt to fulfill her earlier admonition, "Do whatever he tells you" (Jn 2:5).

The word "immaculate" usually means clean and unadulterated, but in this context it also means free, unattached, detached from anything and everything that would divert our attention and energy away from serving the Lord. Mary kept a pure and single-hearted focus on the Lord and his divine will for her, reminding us of Our Lord's promise: "Blessed are the pure in heart, for they shall see God" (Mt 5:8).

Drawing Near to the Heart of Mary

Consecrating ourselves to the Immaculate Heart of Mary should not be done lightly. We need to take time to prayerfully discern and listen with our whole being to the inspirations, promptings, and motivations of the Holy Spirit operating within us. We need to ascertain just what the Lord is trying to tell us. Only after we have discerned what God would have us do should we decide how we are to put it into practice in our daily living.

For example, if we feel drawn to do some kind of penance, we must first decide the nature and extent of what we intend to do. In our first fervor, we may be inclined to be too severe, and may be more demanding than is good for our health. Or we may be inclined to resolve to spend several hours in prayer each day, to the detriment of our family or our mission in life.

Moderation should be our watchword. Do not make resolutions hastily, but spend time in praying for enlightenment and guidance. Remember, prudence is an important virtue. It may be wise to start with resolutions for a definite period of time, then discern the results.

As we strive to hear more precisely what the Lord is asking of us, as Our Lady requests, we begin by making an honest review of our own life. This is not a negative survey of our spiritual life, but rather a means of discovering in what areas we can further our spiritual growth and maturation. Here are a few areas our Blessed Mother at Fatima requested that we live more deeply.

Faith. Is my faith a real, dynamic, operative faith? Is there any area in my life where I find it difficult to place my complete confidence and trust in the Lord to guide me? Am I prepared to offer that area up to him now?

Prayer. Am I faithful in giving the Lord some quality time for prayer each day? Do I strive to offer "ever more intense prayer"? Do I pray daily and fervently for peace in our world? Do I pray daily for the conversion of the world?

Penance. Do I make some sacrifice each day? Do I practice spiritual disciplines such as fasting and self-denial in order to grow to maturity in Christ? Remember, the Lord wants us to be prudent and to avoid any extreme penances that are too difficult to fulfill. He does not want us to be anxious, or to worry that we are not doing enough. Such anxiety is not of God. Seeking the advice of a spiritual director or other spiritually mature person is advisable in this matter if you tend to be overly scrupulous.

Reconciliation. Am I at peace with God, with myself, with all my brothers and sisters? Do I readily and really forgive? Do I always reflect the peace of the Lord by my attitudes, my words, and actions to everyone who crosses my path?

Conversion. Do I need to turn more completely to God by detaching myself from my comforts and hobbies, or from easy compromises with the worldly society in which I live?

Consecration. When she asked that we consecrate ourselves to her Immaculate Heart, Mary was simply asking for a resolve or commitment on our part to live a dedicated Christian way of life, following her example of striving to fulfill the will of God in every aspect of her life.

Each day we must choose to renew our commitment to follow Christ, as echoed in the words of the Morning Offering: "O Jesus, through the Immaculate Heart of Mary I offer you all my prayers, works, joys, and sufferings of this day in union with the Holy Sacrifice of the Mass." In all the events of each day, we seek to find and follow the will of God to the best of our ability, relying on the graces God grants us through the sacraments. May our prayer be the same as the prayer of Jesus: "I have come to do thy will, O God" (Heb 10:7).

There is also a more formal and solemn consecration to Mary recommended by St. Louis de Montfort. This act of consecration should be made only after a longer period of study and prayerful preparation with the guidance of a spiritual director or some other knowledgeable person.

Special Devotional Practices to Consider

Granted the weakness of our human nature, our enthusiasm and resolve to live our consecration daily may wane as we are more and more engrossed in the demands of daily living. To encourage us to persevere in our commitment and consecration to her Immaculate Heart, Mary asked that we adopt a special devotional practice. She made a special request that on the first Saturday of every month we renew our act of consecration, offer Mass and Holy Communion in reparation for sin, and spend fifteen minutes in quiet prayer. This devotion will also assist us in striving for the objectives of the millennial renewal.

The requests Mary made many years ago, at Fatima and elsewhere, are in complete harmony with the objectives of the Great Renewal of the third millennium. May her instructions continue to inspire in all of us, in the words of Pope John Paul II, "a true longing for holiness, a deep desire for conversion and personal renewal."

FIVE

MEDJUGORJE: A CALL TO THE SACRAMENTAL LIFE

"I am the bread of life. Whoever comes to me will never be hungry, and whoever believes in me will never be thirsty."
JOHN 6:35, NRSV

"The primary tasks [of this preparation] include a renewed appreciation of the presence and activity of the Spirit who acts within the Church in the sacraments."
POPE JOHN PAUL II

The fourth of the better-known apparitions of Our Lady began in the village of Medjugorje, Yugoslavia. Mary appeared to six children—four girls and two boys—on June 24, 1981. Her appearances have continued to this day, making them the most frequent Marian appearances in one place.

The Madonna, as she is lovingly called at Medjugorje, illuminates our path to a deeply committed Christian way of life, a way first outlined by her Son, Jesus. Through her messages at Medjugorje, Mary invites us to live a deeper faith, more fervent prayer, personal renewal, sincere conversion, greater penance, and genuine peace. Since these principles are so basic to gospel spirituality, it is not surprising that Pope John Paul II set forth the same objectives in his apostolic letter "The Coming of the Third Millennium."

These guidelines, first followed by the early Christians, have always been the foundation of Christian spirituality. Since we experience peaks and valleys in our striving for perfection, we need to be reminded of the directives Jesus set forth in the Gospel. Our gracious Father sent Mary, our spiritual Mother, to Medjugorje to caution us lest we be influenced by the false ideologies surrounding us and be led astray from the Lord. She also asks us to rekindle our resolve to accept the invitation of her Son when he bids us, "Come, follow me."

Mary, Queen of Peace

Mary identifies herself as the Queen of Peace, eager and anxious to lead us into that peace which the world cannot give. Genuine peace is the fruit of a fourfold relationship. We must be at peace with God; at peace with ourselves by accepting ourselves as we are; at peace with others by manifesting our concern for family, friends, acquaintances; and finally, at peace with our own human nature with its gifts and talents, its limitations and weaknesses. We are at peace with created nature around us with its beauty and productivity, with its rain and sunshine, heat and cold. Our ability to adapt cheerfully will bring us peace.

Be Reconciled with God

In her maternal concern, Mary points out two major avenues to the *shalom*, or peace, that Jesus promised. "The Coming of the

Third Millennium" draws attention to the first of these avenues by calling for "a renewed appreciation and more intense celebration of the Sacrament of Penance in its most profound meaning."[1]

We are to be reconciled with God by seeking his merciful forgiveness and compassionate healing. By his redemptive death Jesus reconciled the whole human race. Lest we see this universal forgiveness as impersonal, however, Jesus instituted the sacrament of reconciliation, in which we meet him personally to be assured of his merciful, forgiving love. At Medjugorje, Our Lady asks us to meet Jesus regularly in this sacrament, hopefully once each month.

Many blessings flow from the sacrament of reconciliation. The most obvious is the one mentioned by G.K. Chesterton, a prominent English convert, when he was asked why he joined the Catholic Church. His ready answer: "To have my sins forgiven." This, of course, is the primary purpose of the sacrament, but it is not the only reason for receiving it.

Meeting Jesus. Through the sacrament of reconciliation we encounter the Person of Jesus, who is present in every sacrament. His presence assures us of his love, mercy, and compassion. Since his love is infinite, and love must give, Jesus is more eager to forgive us than we are to be forgiven. He is pleased when we show our appreciation for this great gift by meeting him regularly in the sacrament. Receiving this sacrament is also a way to acknowledge and affirm who Jesus wants to be in our lives: our Savior and Redeemer.

Receiving healing. Reconciliation is also a powerful channel of healing. We may become discouraged when we fall again and again; we regret that we are not improving in overcoming our weaknesses.

Too often, for example, we may be unkind to someone we dislike, without being able to change. In cases like this we need to look beyond our faults and failings by searching for the underlying problem. Perhaps the person we are treating unkindly is a threat to us—more successful, more affluent, or threatening in some other way. Once we become aware of the reason for our wrongful behavior, we can bring it to the Lord in the sacrament of penance. This will help us receive the healing we need to move out of sinful patterns.

Being transformed. In addition to bringing healing and conversion, the sacrament of reconciliation also helps to transform us into the kind of people the Lord calls us to be. When we know deep in our hearts that we are pardoned, we enjoy genuine peace and tranquillity. This conditions us to bring the peace we have received to our family, friends, and all those who pass along our way.

Persons who live in sin block the divine life and love of the Lord from flowing through them and reaching out to others. Persons who are reconciled to God bring his luminous love into their surroundings through their attitudes and actions.

"Do This in Remembrance of Me"

The second major avenue to peace—also mentioned both at Medjugorje and in the apostolic letter—is the Eucharist. Through this sacrament, "the Savior... continues to offer himself to humanity as the source of divine life."[2] In her appearances at Medjugorje, the Madonna pleaded with us to join her Son in offering the eucharistic celebration frequently and fervently.

We can arrive at a better appreciation of the Mass by recalling some of the reasons why Jesus gave us himself in the Eucharist and bade us: "Do this in remembrance of me" (Lk 22:19).

Gift of love. In the first place the Eucharist assures us of Jesus' boundless love for us. "As the Father has loved me, so have I loved you," Jesus said at the Last Supper. "Abide in my love" (Jn 15:9). The Father's love for Jesus is infinite; likewise, the love of Jesus for us is also infinite.

Love by its very nature wants to be close to the person loved, to share the joys and sorrows of life. The eucharistic sacrifice is a constant reminder of God's immense love, assuring us that we are loved and lovable.

Sign of nearness. Jesus was well aware that since we are human and our thinking so mundane, it would be difficult for us to understand his spiritual presence with us at all times. To help us comprehend his presence more readily, he gave us a tangible sign and symbol in the bread and wine. These items we can see and touch help us to recall his promise: "And lo, I am with you always, to the close of the age" (Mt 28:20).

Offering of self. Our purpose in life is to offer ourselves with all that we are and do to the Lord. The Mass affords us a privileged opportunity to make this oblation of ourselves. The bread and wine symbolize our food and drink, the essentials we need to preserve life. As these gifts are offered at Mass, we offer the Lord our whole lives—good deeds, shortcomings, and all.

Even though our offering may be distracted, halfhearted, or even made reluctantly, Jesus unites it to his own gift; after purifying and sanctifying it, he offers it to the Father in our name. In so doing he adds a tremendous dimension to our gift of self.

Source of refreshment. How correct Jesus was to say, "Apart from me you can do nothing" (Jn 15:5). Along the pathway of life we enjoy many happy and satisfying experiences. Strewn along the way we also encounter heartaches and hardships. When these burdens grow heavy and seemingly intolerable, Jesus comes to our rescue and invites us: "Come to me, all who labour and are heavy laden, and I will give you rest" (Mt 11:28). In the Eucharist Jesus comes to lighten these burdens, worries, and anxieties and fill us with strength and peace by his presence with us.

Power-packed Prayer

In her many messages at Medjugorje, Our Lady asks us repeatedly to pray, pray, pray. She also pleads with us to recognize and offer the Mass as the highest form of prayer that we are privileged to offer. Mary encourages us to make the Mass the very center and heart of our life—which would fulfill one of the objectives of the millennial renewal for "ever more intense prayer."

We will never be able to comprehend the intrinsic mystery of the Eucharist. A few reflections on the different prayers of the Mass, however, will bring us to a deeper appreciation of this sacrament as the most powerful prayer we can offer.

The opening *penitential rite* indicates that all prayer must begin with humility and a sincere acknowledgment of our dependence on the providential care and concern of our loving Father, and of our need for peace and pardon. We begin Mass with this affirmation of our sinfulness so that we may more worthily pray the Mass.

The *Gloria* then allows us to join the whole Body of Christ as together we praise and thank our good God, saying, "Glory to God in the highest." Pondering the infinite goodness of the Lord will make our praise and thanks an "ever more intense prayer."

In the prayers of the *Offertory* we unite our prayer with the prayer of Jesus and are joined by our Mother Mary, all the heavenly hosts, and all the members of the Body of Christ. This adds a tremendous dimension and efficacy to our personal prayer. As an intercessory prayer the Mass is pleasing to the Father, since we plead in the name of Jesus. This is clearly indicated by the conclusions of the principal prayers, for example, "We ask this through Christ our Lord" or "Grant this through our Lord Jesus Christ your Son."

In the specific *petitions* of the Mass we also pray for personal renewal, for reconciliation and unity for all people—our family, acquaintances, community, and, in fact, the whole world. We plead with the Holy Spirit, the source of love and unity, that we may "become one body, one spirit in Christ."

The *sign of peace* reminds us that in his farewell address Jesus promised us genuine peace: "Peace I leave with you; my peace I give to you; not as the world gives" (Jn 14:27). We pray for that peace in the hearts of men and women throughout the world. *Shalom,* the word Jesus used, which is translated by our word "peace," is a prayer for all God's blessings, especially the eternal peace of heaven. After praying for peace, we extend a sign of that prayerful wish to those who are celebrating with us.

Toward the conclusion of Mass, we are commissioned to radiate the love, peace, and joy which our eucharistic Lord shares so graciously with us. In his words of *dismissal* the celebrant urges us to "Go in peace to love and serve the Lord"—to carry God's blessings to all those we meet as we go about our daily round of duties.

Little wonder that Mary appealed to us to make the Mass the very heart and center of our lives. If every Catholic took this call seriously, what vast strides we would make toward the total revitalization we are eagerly awaiting in the coming millennium! The determination of each individual person to strive for the objectives of the renewal will contribute to its anticipated success. Failing to respond will diminish the level of success.

The requests of the Madonna of Medjugorje, like her other appearances already mentioned, lay the groundwork for our entering into the Great Jubilee. To fulfill our role will require discipline and perseverance, but the joy and satisfaction we experience will be rewarding. In the Lord's inscrutable plan for this age, we each have a part to play. Let us play it to the best of our ability, for the Lord is counting on us.

Mary, Mother
of the Church

"Here is your Mother."
John 19:25, NRSV

*"We believe that the Mother of God, the Mother
of the Church, continues in heaven to exercise
her maternal role on behalf of the
members of Christ."*
Pope Paul VI

Mary, the Mother of Jesus and our Mother, has been known and loved by Christians down through the ages. She has been accorded very many different titles—far too many to enumerate—which indicate her maternal concern for every phase of our spiritual and physical well-being.

On November 21, 1964, at the end of the third session of the Second Vatican Council, Mary received the title "Mother of the Church." This all-inclusive title embraces the others by which Mary is known. As Pope Paul VI declares in *The Catechism of the Catholic Church*:

"The Virgin Mary... is acknowledged and honored as being truly the Mother of God and of the Redeemer.... She is 'clearly the mother of the members of Christ'… since she has by her charity joined in bringing about the birth of believers in the Church, who are members of its head."

"Mary, Mother of Christ, Mother of the Church."[1]

To encourage a widespread devotion to Mary, the Mother of the Church, a special Mass was composed. It is entitled, "The Blessed Virgin Mary, Image and Mother of the Church."

Four Moments of Mary's Motherhood

The Preface of this special Mass recalls four particular moments in the history of salvation in which Mary fulfilled her maternal role, entitling her to be honored as the Mother of the Church. The first of these moments took place at the time of the Annunciation. The Preface recalls it with this prayer:

She received your Word in the purity of her heart, and, conceiving in her virgin womb, gave birth to our Savior and so nurtured the Church at its very beginning.

The second revelation of Mary's motherly role was on the hill of Calvary, where Jesus handed over his Mother to us as our very own: "Here is your Mother." The words of the Preface remind us:

She accepted God's parting gift of love as she stood beneath the cross and so became the mother of all those who were brought to life through the death of her only Son.

The third mention of this maternal role centers on Mary's presence with the apostles in the Upper Room after the Ascension, where they prayed fervently for the outpouring of the Holy Spirit.

She joined her prayers with those of the apostles, as together they awaited the coming of Your Spirit and so became the perfect pattern of the Church at prayer.

The fourth reason Mary is rightly called the Mother of the Church has to do with her Assumption into heaven. The Preface puts it this way:

Raised to the glory of heaven, she cares for the pilgrim Church with a mother's love, following its progress homeward until the day of the Lord dawns in splendor.

In all of the episodes mentioned in the Preface to this special Mass, Mary responded to the will of God by offering herself humbly and graciously. At every step she cooperated with God's salvific plan. How rightly she deserves to be called the Mother of the Church!

With the Infant Church, with Today's Church

Mary proved her deep motherly concern for the Church from the moment of its birth, as she gathered with the disciples and holy women in the Upper Room. Their ten-day vigil awaiting the outpouring of the Holy Spirit that Jesus had promised was a response to the Lord's command:

While staying with them he charged them not to depart Jerusalem, but to wait for the promise of the Father, which, he said, "You heard from me, for John baptized with water, but before many days you shall be baptized with the Holy Spirit."

ACTS 1:4-5

With his usual attention to detail, St. Luke is careful to note that Mary, the Mother of Jesus, was there with the group: "All these with one accord devoted themselves to prayer, together with the women and Mary the mother of Jesus, and with his brethren" (Acts 1:14).

Just as Mary prayed fervently for the outpouring of the Holy Spirit on the infant Church, she continues her powerful intercession for the Church today, and for each one of us as members of the Church. Mary experienced the power of the Holy Spirit in her own life. She witnessed the transforming power of the Holy Spirit in the lives of the apostles as they launched out to bring the Good News of salvation to the whole world. Thus Mary understands how very much we too need the Spirit's divine enlightenment and transforming power if we are to do our part to revitalize the Christian way of life in our own world.

This is why Mary's role as the Mother of the Church is vitally significant in the Christian renewal we anticipate. Since we are all members of the Church, the spiritual Body of Christ, Mary is eager to help us by her powerful prayers and to guide our steps by the example of her own lifestyle. In his apostolic letter, the Holy Father assures us that Mary is the Star that will guide us through every stage of the Great Renewal. His words reflect the confidence he has in Mary's powerful influence.

I entrust this responsibility of the whole Church to the maternal intercession of Mary, Mother of the Redeemer. She, the Mother of fairest love, will be for Christians on the way to the Great Jubilee of the Third Millennium the Star which safely guides their steps to the Lord.[2]

Spiritual Mother of the Body of Christ

The Body of Christ is present in the world today. Jesus lives in all the members that make up his Body. Every person is either an actual member or a potential member of the Body of Christ.

We who are members of the Church were initiated into his Body at the time of our baptism. In this sacramental rite the Father adopted us as his daughters and sons, and the Holy Spirit came to dwell within us, making us his very special temple. Jesus, too, dwells within us in his risen, glorified life. This divine indwelling makes us the Body of Christ, a member of the family of God and brothers and sisters to one another.

As the Mother of this Body, the Church, Mary is deeply concerned about each one of us, her spiritual children. Like our natural mother, Mary is lovingly protective of our spiritual and temporal welfare. We have seen how God has permitted his Mother to appear on many different occasions and in many different places to caution and to warn us of the dangers which threaten to rob us of the peace, happiness, and tranquillity which the Lord wants us to enjoy.

There is indeed much that threatens the Body of Christ in our world today. Reflect for a moment on how greatly the Church is suffering in our society. Violence, injustice, greed, poverty, immorality, and a widespread disregard for human rights are only some of the ailments afflicting the members of the Body of Christ. These afflictions are caused by our rejection of God and his way of life.

Why have people turned away from God in such large numbers? Why do they no longer accompany him? There are many and various reasons; they result from a widespread weakening of faith which has generated an attitude of indifference toward spiritual values.

We have made such vast strides in technology that some people feel they no longer have need of God. We have become self-sufficient and sophisticated, relegating God to the background or out of our lives entirely. The philosophy of personalism—pushed to extremes, with an insistence on our own individual rights—has made us a greedy, self-centered society that is indifferent to the rights of others. Ethical relativism and individualism have undermined our objective standards of morality. And much suffering has been caused by man's inhumanity to man.

Needed: Worldwide Conversion

Our sick society is in dire need of a wholesale conversion, a universal turning to God. This is what we are eagerly anticipating in the coming millennium. In times of crisis, our heavenly Father will not desert us. He uses extraordinary means to arrest our attention and lead us back to his way of life.

As we have already mentioned, one of the unusual means that God is using to caution and warn of the impending danger are the frequent appearances of our Blessed Mother. From Guadalupe to Lourdes, on to Fatima and now Medjugorje (to mention only a few of Mary's many appearances), our solicitous Mother is earnestly appealing to us to recognize the impending disaster to souls which could result if we continue to pursue our godless trend.

In all her appearances, our Blessed Mother pleads for the conversion of the whole world, especially the members of her Son's Body. She continually reminds us of the program for conversion which Jesus set forth in the gospel. Her requests include prayer, penance, fasting, reconciliation, a deeper faith commitment, and, above all, "ever more intense prayer." To attain this end a process of conversion must take place in our lives.

Conversion has a twofold connotation. It means primarily a turning to the Lord. For most of us, it means a more complete turning to the Lord by recommitting our lives more fully. This can be accomplished by striving to know the Lord as a personal, loving God who loves us with an unconditional love. We will increase our heart knowledge of Jesus through "devotional readings" of the gospel, listening as he reveals himself to us. Only when we know him with our heart can we love him. Our deeper commitment, then, consists of doing everything Jesus asks of us, as a means of expressing our love for him in return for the love he is lavishing upon us.

For those who are no longer accompanying Jesus, conversion may mean a sincere turning away from a life of sin and infidelity and turning toward God. This means acknowledging sinfulness and seeking forgiveness through the sacramental rite of reconciliation which Jesus himself has instituted for us.

As the Refuge of Sinners, our Mother Mary is deeply concerned about all those who have wandered in the mist. She does not want a single drop of the precious blood of her Son to have been spilled in vain. Through her powerful intercession she has guided many who have strayed, leading them back to the loving embrace of her Son.

Is it unrealistic to pray for the conversion of the whole world? Not if Mary is interceding and working for it too! At any rate, the conversion of the whole world begins with our own conversion, and then the conversion of those whose lives we may influence.

Prophetic Image

Many artists through the years have drawn inspiration from Mary and have given us works of art in various media—painting, sculpture, music, and so on—which provide us with much inspiration, motivation, and enjoyment.

One of these treasured images is the masterpiece of Michelangelo, the Pietà. This immortal sculpture is prophetic of Mary's continued and universal maternal solicitude for the Church in the world today.

The Pietà portrays the scene we contemplate at the thirteenth station along the Way of the Cross. Jesus has been tenderly taken down from the cross by Joseph of Arimathea and Nicodemus, and laid in the waiting arms of his Mother. Not only for its artistry is this work of art loved and appreciated by millions around the world, but also for the message it conveys: the Pietà reminds us that Mary is the Mother of the spiritual Body of Christ, the Church.

Get a picture of the Pietà, if you can, or at least think about this image for a few moments. Be with Mary as she lovingly receives the lifeless body of Jesus into her outstretched arms. Some years before, Mary had pressed his little body to her heart. Throughout those hidden years in Nazareth, she must have embraced her Son countless times. Michelangelo's sculpture portrays her receiving his battered and bloody body, cold and clammy in death. We can well visualize Mary wiping away the blood, dirt, and spittle as she tenderly touches every wound and laceration while she relives the dreadful suffering he endured.

Mary's Ongoing Mission

This timeless masterpiece of Michelangelo speaks to and about our society today. Our faith enables us to envision a similar image in our modern world.

Just as Mary, Mother of Jesus, lovingly tends the broken body of her Son, so does Mary, Mother of the Church, take the wounded, bleeding spiritual Body of Christ into her arms; again, she touches every wound, every laceration, every bruise, every hurt.

Our gracious Mother is deeply concerned about every individual member and every potential member of the Body of Christ. She is anxious about all those who are lost in anger, lack of faith, doubt, indifference, or ignorance.

Mary hears the objections of those who say: "This is a hard saying; who can listen to it?" (Jn 6:60). Mary sees the children who do not have any knowledge of Jesus' great love for them. "Let the little children come to me, and do not hinder them" (Mt 19:14), Jesus pleaded—but many children are not being brought to him, and Mary's heart is burdened for them. Mary experienced in her own life the truth of Jesus' statement: "Apart from me you can do nothing" (Jn 15:5), yet she knows how many there are who find no place in their lives for God, nor ever seek his guidance. She is concerned for them, as well as for those who do not understand the words that she herself lived by: "If you love me, you will keep my commandments" (Jn 14:15).

Mary regrets to hear some of her children say, "God's commandments are too restrictive for our times and they rob us of our freedom." They excuse their conduct by maintaining: "God did not mean *me*. He understands that my particular situation is different." Mary grieves that they have adopted a standard of relativism which they affirm is more relevant in our modern age than God's commands.

These are some of the wounds and scars which the Body of Christ, the Church, is suffering in our society today. As a loving Mother, Mary is fervently imploring the Holy Spirit to pour out his love upon her wayward children and endow them with an abundance of the grace of conversion. As the "Star which safely guides us to the Lord," she is praying that her own example may draw them back to the Lord.

Three Avenues of Healing

Mary's maternal healing comes through three different avenues, three aspects of her example of holiness.

Mary's whole life is a paragon of *faith*. When we as a Church strive to renew and strengthen our faith under Mary's guidance, many of our fears, disappointments, anxieties, and fractured relationships will be healed. Our healing will touch other members of the Church.

Our Blessed Mother's *total commitment* will inspire and encourage us to be faithful to our own commitment as members of the Body of Christ. We will hold fast regardless of the uncertainty, dissatisfaction, or discouragement, as well as the fears, doubts, or misgivings, that may loom up during this critical time of transition. May Mary's memorable words rest in our minds and hearts: "Behold, I am the handmaid of the Lord; let it be to me according to your word" (Lk 1:38).

Third, as we strive to imitate Mary's dedicated *life of prayer,* we will establish a deeper, richer relationship with Jesus abiding with us and within us. Mary found much strength and direction in prayer. That is why she urges us to "ever more intense prayer." Mary's maternal admonition is brief but direct: "Do whatever he tells you" (Jn 2:5). Only in prayer will we be able to hear what Jesus is telling us.

Mary's Maternal Role in the Church

As the Mother of the Church and our Mother, Mary is the guiding Star who not only leads us into every phase of the millennial renewal, but supports and encourages us along the way as we strive to accept the challenge and fulfill our own role in the Great Renewal. Her entire lifestyle is a perfect pattern for our emulation. As our guiding Star, she illumines the pathway to the total revitalization of a genuine, committed Christian way of life. Here are a few areas in which her influence is felt.

Mary's dynamic faith is a light in the widespread crisis in faith afflicting the Church and the world. Her undaunted faith will enkindle and increase our own faith as we journey through the ups and downs of life.

Mary's intense love of God teaches us how to respond to the Lord's limitless love for us by willingly accepting whatever comes into our life, both good and bad.

Mary's quiet contemplative prayer posture urges us to relax more frequently with the Lord, to be alone with him in the quiet wordless prayer of the heart.

As the Queen of Peace, Mary demonstrates the requisites for attaining that peace which the world cannot give. Her own peace of mind and heart is a beacon for our daily living.

Mary, the heart of that happy home in Nazareth, is deeply concerned about the deterioration of family life in our society. She prays constantly that peace and harmony may reign in every household as each family draws closer to the Lord. Her powerful intercession will draw dysfunctional families into the embrace of God's boundless love.

As the Refuge of Sinners, our Mother's powerful prayers will influence many calloused hearts and gradually lead them to recognize and accept the forgiving, healing love of God for them.

Since Mary is our caring, concerned Mother, we can be certain that she will be with us when the Lord calls us to our eternal reward. Have we not prayed countless times: "Pray for us sinners, now and at the hour of our death"? Our prayer will not go unanswered.

Mary's principal role in the anticipated revitalization of the Christian way of life is to bring us to Jesus. He will do the rest. Our watchword, then, as we approach the third millennium: To Jesus through Mary!

PART II

LESSONS FROM THE LIFE OF MARY

In the second part of this book we contemplate Mary's life. As the story unfolds, it becomes a perfect pathway encouraging us to follow in Mary's footprints on our journey into the third millennium.

SEVEN

MARY: MODEL OF DISCERNMENT AND OBEDIENCE
The Early Life of Mary Through the Annunciation

"Give me understanding, that I may keep thy law."
PSALMS 119:34

Mary "conceived the Incarnate word by the power of the Holy Spirit and then... allowed herself to be guided by his interior activity."
POPE JOHN PAUL II

The expectations of the third millennium have enkindled within us a vibrant hope for an important revitalization of the Christian way of life for ourselves and our society. We cannot passively wait for the fruits of this renewal to come to us, however. We are called to act, to fulfill a precise role to make the renewal a reality.

But what is our role? The apostolic letter "The Coming of the Third Millennium" describes it as a twofold commission that God has given each one of us for our earthly pilgrimage. We are first to *review our personal relationship with the Lord* in order to determine how to deepen and enrich our union with him. We are advised to have "a true longing for holiness, a deep desire for conversion and a personal renewal in a context of ever more intense prayer."[1]

The second phase of our mission is to *establish a "solidarity with one's neighbor, especially the most needy."*[2] Love of neighbor requires us to be concerned about both the spiritual and material welfare of our brothers and sisters who come into our life.

To meet this challenge we are to ascertain whether we are attuned to the promptings of the Holy Spirit within us, for we will accomplish our twofold mission only as we are alert to his leading. This requires the Spirit's special gift of discernment (see 1 Cor 12:10).

Discernment is a process by which we try to determine precisely what God wishes us to do in a given situation. At some time in our life each of us has thought or said, "I wish I knew what God expects me to do," or, "I wonder how I should handle this problem." Discernment means not only making a prudent judgment or arriving at a definite decision or mode of action in such cases, but doing so in light of God's purposes. Discernment is primarily concerned with discovering God's will in our life.

Even though we have a free will, we are often influenced by certain impulses, promptings, and inclinations urging us into action. Since we are uncertain about their origin, we may be apprehensive about implementing them until we can verify their source. Discernment helps us to ascertain if these promptings are emanating from the Holy Spirit, from a personal desire latent within us, or possibly from a machination of the devil, who seeks to derail us on our spiritual journey.

The procedure for discerning God's will in most matters consists of several steps: taking our concern to the Lord in listening prayer, striving to develop an objective and receptive frame of mind, sharing our problem with a competent person (often a spiritual director or mentor), and finally, reaching a conclusion. If our decision is in tune with God's will, we will enjoy genuine peace.

There are times in life that call for extended periods of

discernment, times when we face important decisions which might change the whole course of our life. A young person may be agonizing over God's will in regard to their vocation in life. Should they prepare for a business or professional career? Are they called to the married state? Could they possibly have a vocation to the priesthood or sisterhood? A husband and father may be deeply concerned about knowing God's will about his job. Should he accept that promotion if it entails moving his family to another city?

There are no universal answers to such questions, of course, but whether the discernment process is shorter or longer, we can count on receiving guidance from the Holy Spirit. We can also draw inspiration from the example of two ideal models: Jesus and Mary his Mother.

Jesus: Our Model of Discernment

Since good models can assist us greatly in our mundane pursuits, how much more valuable are they on our unchartered journey to a deeper, more personal relationship with the Lord. There are many men and women whose lifestyles give evidence of having discerned well the will of God in their daily duties. Their example can be a great boon in our own discerning process. We are inspired, encouraged, and guided as we reflect on their way of life.

Our greatest model of discernment is, of course, Jesus himself. He was always attuned to the Father's will. Even before Jesus' Incarnation, the psalmist foretold that the Messiah who would eventually come into the world would fulfill the will of the Lord precisely: "I delight to do thy will, O my God; thy law is within my heart" (Ps 40:8). During his sojourn on earth, Jesus was always singleminded in fulfilling his Father's will, even in the slightest detail. His words are unmistakably clear: "For I have come down from heaven, not to do my own will, but the will of him who sent me" (Jn 6:38).

To ascertain the Father's will exactly, Jesus used a process of discernment. We see this most clearly on the many occasions when Jesus prayed that he might know what the Father wanted him to do in a given situation. Before choosing the twelve apostles, "he went out into the hills to pray; and all night he continued in prayer to God" (Lk 6:12).

As his teaching mission was drawing to a close, Jesus took his three favorite apostles up on Mount Tabor; there he prayed to know if this was the time for him to go to Jerusalem to begin his redemptive suffering and death. Jesus also prayed for the strength to accept whatever redemptive suffering might be demanded of him. His final submission to the Father echoed from the cross as "Jesus, crying with a loud voice, said: 'Father, into thy hands I commit my spirit'" (Lk 23:46).

Jesus left us a lofty example of discerning and following the Father's will. Well aware that we might be overwhelmed and even discouraged at the prospect of striving to emulate him, he also left us another help for discerning the will of God, another model, companion, and helpmate on our journey through life: his Mother.

Mary: Our Mother and Model

Mary is our model in all the facets of daily living, but especially does she show us the way in discerning and fulfilling the Lord's will in her life. Her whole way of life is a perfect pattern for us to follow. Jesus therefore urges us to imitate her example, adopt her attitudes, form her mind and heart within ourselves.

As we examine the discernment process, it is profitable for us to reflect on several aspects of Mary's life. First of all, we will consider her special relationship with the Holy Spirit, out of which flowed the elements that always enabled Mary to discern exactly what God wished her to do. We will then consider the episode of

Mary's life which perhaps best illustrates her perfect discernment and obedience: the Annunciation.

Sinless Temple of the Holy Spirit

The Holy Spirit was operative within Mary from the very moment of her conception. He sanctified her by preapplying the fruits of the redemption to her, thus preserving her immaculate soul free from every vestige or defect of original sin. From the first moment of her life Mary was a perfect temple of the Holy Spirit, who was dynamic and operative in her sinless soul.

Since Mary was immaculately conceived and preserved from all sin throughout her lifetime, the Holy Spirit could mold and transform her freely. Mary's recorded words in Scripture are extremely sparse, but what we can see of her way of life speaks eloquently to us of this deep personal relationship with the Holy Spirit. Throughout her entire earthly sojourn, the Spirit inspired, guided, comforted, and supported Mary in her unique mission.

Filled with the Spirit, Mary was always attentive to the various media through which the Lord communicated his plan to her and also invited her to accept the role he had envisioned for her. God was pleased to reveal his plan to Mary in many different ways, both directly and indirectly: through the words of Scripture— especially the prophecies—and through the angel Gabriel.

The interior promptings and dynamic presence of the Holy Spirit within her empowered Mary to discern God's will in all the events of her earthly journey. Mary's whole being, illumined by the Holy Spirit, recognized God's designs in Gabriel's surprising announcement, in the privations of Bethlehem, the frightening escape into Egypt, the poverty of Nazareth, the loneliness during the public ministry of Jesus, the painful oblation on Calvary, the ecstatic joy of the Resurrection, and the lonely sojourn after the ascension of Jesus into heaven.

As we contemplate the transforming power of the Holy Spirit in the life of Mary, we will discover her as a perfect model as we strive to discern God's will in our own lives. Mary's unflinching response to the Lord is a source of great inspiration for us.

Be assured, as our Mother she understands our self-will and hesitation, our doubts and fears, our lack of faith and trust in the Lord. Through her powerful intercession Mary will be constantly at our side to comfort and encourage, to reassure and assist us. Her maternal advice is always the same: "Do whatever he tells you" (Jn 2:5). The same Holy Spirit who overshadowed Mary is present within us and will help us to know, understand, and do whatever he tells us.

"But I'm not like Mary!" some object. "*I* was not conceived without sin! How can I imitate her discernment and obedience?"

Baptism is what makes this possible. The rich spiritual gifts conferred upon us through this sacrament make it one of the most important events in our life. Through Baptism the Father adopts us as his sons and daughters and we become members of the Body of Christ. Baptism initiates us into the life of the Holy Spirit. We become the temple of the Spirit, as St. Paul repeatedly reminds us: "Do you not know that you are God's temple, and that God's Spirit dwells in you?" (1 Cor 3:16; see also 6:19; 2 Cor 6:16).

Jesus promised us that the Spirit "remains with you and will be within you" (Jn 14:17) and that "he will guide you to all truth" (Jn 16:13). The presence of the Holy Spirit is indeed dynamic and operative within us, strengthening and encouraging us in all the happenings of our earthly pilgrimage. The Spirit enlightens and leads us through the myriad tasks of every day, guiding us in all that we undertake through his gift of "discernment of spirits." (1 Cor 12:10).

The dynamism of the Holy Spirit within us is limited only by the degree of our receptivity and by the extent of our cooperation with his gifts and graces. Sin is the prime obstacle to his activity in us. The more ardently we strive to avoid sin, the more effectively will the Holy Spirit transform us, enabling us to discern God's will in our daily living.

Three effects of the Spirit's inner transformation, in particular, are crucial for discerning God's will: union with God, prayerfulness, and love that leads to perfect obedience. In Mary these qualities are perfectly realized.

In Union with God

Mary lived her life totally in union with God. Her mind and heart were always in tune with the Lord. She was ever aware of his presence and his mysterious plans for her.

Keeping her focus on the Lord, she eagerly fulfilled every detail of the law of the Lord as it was known at that time. Scripture informs us that Mary presented Jesus in the temple, "as it is written in the law of the Lord" (Lk 2:23) and that every year she and Joseph went to Jerusalem for the festival of the Passover, as the law required (see Lk 2:41).

In her home in Nazareth, with Jesus in her arms and later at her side, Mary lived constantly in the presence of the Lord. Her intimate union with Jesus, like her union with the Holy Spirit, enabled her to discern God's will all the days of her life.

Though we cannot travel back in time to live with the Holy Family in Nazareth, we too can keep ourselves in union with the Lord and put on the mind and heart of Jesus. We do this by keeping our focus on him and walking his way of life, avoiding anything that may lead us away from him. The psalmist offers us a few simple directives:

Happy are those
    who do not follow the advice of the wicked,
or take the path that sinners tread,
    or sit in the seat of scoffers;

but their delight is in the law of the Lord
and on his law they meditate day and night.

PSALMS 1:1-2, NRSV

Our union with Jesus, fashioned like Mary's, will deepen as we come to know him as a personal God who loves us with an unconditional love, inspires and motivates us, enlightens and strengthens us, fills us with his mercy and compassion. As we contemplate Jesus as he reveals himself in the Gospel, we can expect our will to become attuned to his will. Gradually his mind and heart will be formed within us. Union with God is thus the first major step in helping us discern what God is asking from us.

The Prayerfulness of Mary

Mary's prayerfulness guided her in discerning the will of the Lord. As Mary pondered and reflected upon the mysterious working of God in her life, her prayer for the most part became a quiet prayer of listening.

Mary spent much time in silence and solitude—not an empty, noncommunicative silence, but a silence of being quietly absorbed in the love of the Holy Spirit present within her. This posture of listening with her heart kept Mary attentive to the inspirations and insights of the Holy Spirit communicating with her.

For us too this method of wordless prayer is extremely helpful in the process of trying to discern what the Lord may be asking of us. Thomas Merton assures us that this prayer of the heart, or contemplation, gives us insights which we could not know otherwise. As we pray for guidance in discerning his will, God may not give us specific directions, nor a step-by-step procedure to follow; he does enlighten us, however, giving us the grace to comprehend his will more clearly.

Here too Mary shows us the way and invites us to follow her in these days of millennial renewal. In his apostolic letter, the Holy Father draws our attention to Mary's example of docility and silent attentiveness:

> Mary, who conceived the Incarnate Word by the power of the Holy Spirit and then in the whole of her life allowed herself to be guided by his interior activity, will be contemplated and imitated during this year above all as the woman who was docile to the voice of the Spirit, a woman of silence and attentiveness....[3]

Mary's life was a continuum of giving her consent to the inspirations and guidance of the Holy Spirit. In her quiet prayer, Mary was able to discern and recognize the promptings of the Holy Spirit. This enabled her to respond positively and willingly to the Lord's divine will in the special vocation to which she was called.

May we contemplate and imitate Mary's prayerful attentiveness and docility so that we too may be able to fulfill our role in these precious days of the great Jubilee.

Mary's Love and Discernment

Discernment is the sensitivity given to those who love the Lord with all their hearts to seek God's will for them, especially his will of preference—what will please him most. Discernment cannot be separated from love. If we truly love the Lord, we will more easily recognize his will; we will be more generously disposed to fulfill it.

Here again Mary sets the pace. She loved the Lord with a love that has never been excelled by any other creature on earth. The influx of God's love into her soul empowered Mary to rise above the self-centeredness which plagues so many of us. Mary was eager to know what would please God, and her unselfishness kept her alert to his inspirations and the movement of grace. Furthermore, Mary's great love gave her keen insight into God's mysterious plans. When she discerned God's will for her, she accepted it unhesitatingly, with complete trust and confidence.

Of course, Mary's unique love stems from her sinlessness, which gave her an unlimited capacity to receive the outpouring of divine love which the Holy Spirit showered upon her. But the Holy Spirit also loves each one of us, sinful though we may be, with an infinite love. He who is the very source of love stands ready to shower it upon us too: "God's love has been poured into our hearts through the Holy Spirit who has been given to us" (Rom 5:5).

As we open our hearts to divine love, our love for God will grow strong and we will long to please him. The Holy Spirit will enkindle within us an ardent desire to fulfill the Lord's will to the best of our ability. Motivated by love like Mary, we will be more sensitive to God's voice, ever eager to respond willingly and graciously to whatever the Lord asks.

The Annunciation—Perfect YES

The Annunciation is perhaps the event of Mary's life which most clearly reveals and highlights the perfect discernment and obedience that the Holy Spirit worked in her.

Not for herself alone was Mary preserved from sin, thereby enjoying a more intimate and personal union with the Lord than any other human being has ever known. This prerogative was accorded Mary so that she might be a worthy dwelling for Jesus, the Second Person of the Holy Trinity. Throughout Mary's tender years the Spirit had prepared and empowered the young girl for the privileged mission of becoming the Mother of the Messiah, our Savior and Redeemer. During this time Mary must have kept her heart attuned to the promptings of the Spirit dwelling within her.

This training in discernment enabled Mary to say her yes to all that God asked of her through the angel Gabriel. Somehow, without understanding it fully, Mary grasped the truth of the angel's announcement: that through the unique and extraordinary work of the Spirit, she was to become the Mother of the Messiah.

Mary did not hesitate. She did not ask for any guarantees, nor offer any objections. She asked only one question—and that was to determine more precisely how she was to carry out God's will: "How can this be, since I have no husband?" When the angel assured her, "The Holy Spirit will come upon you and the power of the Most High will overshadow you," Mary gave her complete consent. Her loving obedience is captured in those memorable words which have reechoed down through the centuries: "Let it be to me according to your word" (Lk 1:34-35, 38).

Was there ever a greater faith, trust, and confidence manifested in God's mysterious way?

Being invited to become the Mother of the Messiah was a great, a unique privilege indeed! But we must not forget that it was also a challenge, even for Mary. Mary was sinless, but that did not deprive her of her humanness. She was a human being with all the feelings and emotions we experience; she had her moments of pain and sorrow, joy and happiness, like any other normal person. Recalling this fact will give us greater empathy with Mary and also a deeper appreciation of all the difficulties she had to face.

The major difficulty and challenge was that Mary was asked to become a mother in the most unheard-of way. Never had it been recorded in the annals of human history that a child was born without a natural father. What a challenge to faith!

Mary had to face another problem. We must remember that she was only espoused to Joseph, and not yet married. In the culture of that day pregnancy outside of wedlock was not tolerated. A woman could even be stoned to death for it. How then was Mary to bring her child into the world, and how were she and her child to survive?

Perhaps Mary was thinking of Joseph too. According to the laws and customs of that time, if a man married a pregnant woman, he would be cut off from Israel forever. What terrible suffering and disappointment for Joseph. How could he be expected to understand Mary's pregnancy, the mysterious working of the Lord in her life? Mary had no guarantees that God would vindicate her in a way that preserved her reputation. (And she probably did not suspect that God would send an angel to reassure and guide Joseph.)

In Mary's immediate generous response we see the discernment and obedience that flowed from her relationship with the Holy Spirit. As the bishops in the Second Vatican Council said of Mary, in the "Dogmatic Constitution on the Church":

> Embracing God's salvific will with a full heart and impeded by no sin, she devoted herself totally as a handmaid of the Lord to the person and work of her Son, under him and with him by the grace of almighty God, serving the mystery of redemption.[4]

This, then, is the goal to which Mary calls us: single-hearted attentiveness to God's desires and total abandonment to his plans. Mary's maternal concern is that we too may be generous and faithful in giving ourselves totally and perseveringly to God with all we think, do, and say.

Mary's openness to the Holy Spirit, her prayerfulness and committed love make her an ideal model for us as we seek to discern and respond to the will of the Lord. We can begin to follow her example by heeding what her Son would tell us:

- "And lo, I am with you always" (Mt 28:20). I am always faithful to this promise. Take a little breather regularly throughout the day to recall my presence with you and "abide in my love" (Jn 15:9).

- Follow the example of my Mother by being open and cooperative at all times to the promptings of the Holy Spirit, who is dynamic and operative within you.

- Spend time with me daily in wordless prayer, resting in my love with a heart that will listen to what I want to tell you.

- As my Mother and Elizabeth conversed about the mysterious workings of the Spirit in their lives, you would do well to share with your spiritual director or some other competent person the direction the Holy Spirit seems to be leading you.

EIGHT

MARY: MODEL OF PRAYER
The Visitation and the Birth of Jesus

"Pray constantly, give thanks in all circumstances."
1 THESSOLONIANS 5:17-18

*"Many have entered the Kingdom without the sacraments.
None have entered without prayer."*
KARL RAHNER

The powerful transformation we are eagerly anticipating during this third millennium calls all Christians to a more vibrant faith, a more complete conversion, and a richer, more personal relationship with Jesus. "The Coming of the Third Millennium" points out that these changes will be brought to fruition only "in a context of ever more intense prayer."[1] The effectiveness of our efforts to restore a more dedicated Christian way of life for ourselves and our society will depend to a great extent on the intensity of our prayer and the prayers of all people of good will.

Prayer is primarily giving God our loving presence by offering him prime time, our undivided attentiveness, and willingness to accept and respond to whatever he may ask of us. Again, as we saw in the last chapter, Jesus himself shows us how to do this and sets the pace for us.

Throughout his public ministry, Jesus often went off to a mountain, a desert place, or an olive grove to be absorbed in prayer with his Father. His prayer was characterized by a total oblation of himself: "I have come to do thy will, O God" (Heb 10:7). From his first breath in Bethlehem to his last gasp on the cross, he gave himself totally to the Father's will, as his final words attest: "Father, into thy hands I commit my spirit" (Lk 23:46). Jesus teaches us, his disciples, to pray with a purified heart and also with a lively persevering faith that our prayer may be heard.

Our Companion in Prayer

As we seek to prepare for the third millennium by becoming a person of "ever more intense prayer," we do not have to drift about alone and uncertain, with only a few general directives to lead us into prayer. We have a companion in the person of our Blessed Mother herself, a woman of prayer.

The Church has always encouraged us to have recourse to the communion of saints, assuring us that they are our companions in prayer. Jesus himself proved the intercessory power of Mary's prayer at the wedding feast in Cana. Even though the time of his public ministry had not yet begun, Jesus responded to Mary's plea, "They have no wine," by working his first miracle (Jn 2:3ff).

In the description of Mary's many appearances around the world, we saw that Mary is always pleading for us to "pray, pray, pray." As we concentrate on Mary's request, we discover that she is not necessarily asking for more and more prayers or for a longer time in prayer; rather, she is encouraging us to enter into the deeper, more contemplative life of prayer manifested in Mary's own lifestyle. She realizes that it will not be easy for us to pray consistently and devoutly at all times. As a gracious Mother, Mary is eager and anxious to teach us to pray and to show us by her own example.

Many of us can recall how patiently our good mothers taught us to pray when we were children. I remember well how persever-ingly my own mother taught us children how to pray the rosary. In those days there was much more family ironing to do than today, when so many of the new materials drip dry. As my mother did the family ironing, she stationed us siblings on the floor around the ironing board while she taught us the prayers of the rosary. This was a rather unusual classroom-oratory, but a practical one.

Mary, our spiritual Mother, has her own ways of teaching and leading us into prayer: by her urgent requests in her frequent appearances, by her own example, and also by what we discover in Scripture about her prayer life. There are many dimensions to Mary's prayer life. A brief reflection on some of these, especially on those that stand out in two episodes of Mary's life—her visit to Elizabeth and the birth of Jesus—will assist our efforts to become people of deeper prayer.

Praise and Thanksgiving

Immediately after the Annunciation, Mary must have felt very much alone with her secret. Joseph, a just and God-fearing man, would not be able to relate to such incredible happenings. The vil-lagers would immediately ostracize her if she even tried to explain the workings of the Spirit in her life. How Mary must have wanted to talk to someone about what had happened to her, to share her experience of God's overwhelming goodness!

Then Mary remembered: God's mysterious designs were also at work in her kinswoman Elizabeth, nearly a hundred miles away. Immediately she "set out and went with haste" to visit Elizabeth (Lk 1:39). Elizabeth's faith and gratitude to God immediately manifested themselves when Mary appeared on her doorstep. Her strong faith confirmed Mary's faith. Her praise of Mary was an expression of praise for the God who had worked so powerfully in her:

> Blessed are you among women, and blessed is the fruit of your womb. And why is this granted me, that the Mother of my Lord should come to me?... Blessed is she who believed that there would be a fulfillment of what was spoken to her from the Lord.   LUKE 1:42-43, 45

Filled with joy and gratitude for the miraculous workings of God in her own life as well as in the life of Elizabeth, Mary burst forth in her memorable canticle:

> My soul magnifies the Lord
>   and my spirit rejoices in God my Savior,
> for he has looked with favor
>   on the lowliness of his servant.
> Surely, from now on all
>   all generations will call me blessed;
> for the Mighty One has done great things for me,
>   and holy is his name.   LUKE 1:46-49, NRSV

Mary's hymn of praise and thanksgiving to God "who has done great things for me" echoes down through the centuries. We rejoice with her and praise God, whose bounty we ourselves enjoy with every breath we take.

Mary's song of praise gives us occasion to reflect on our own gratefulness to the Lord. Are we as thankful as we should be for all he has given us? Do we realize that we are called to have grateful hearts? How disappointing is our response compared to what God has given us. Jesus healed ten lepers, but only one returned to thank him: "Were not ten cleansed?" Jesus asked. "Where are the other nine?" (Lk 17:17).

With Mary as our model and companion, let us resolve to give God his due. Then our praise and thanksgiving will be radiated in our whole life and will hasten the Great Renewal we are anticipating in this millennium.

Praying with Scripture

Mary's visit to Elizabeth reveals another important element of her prayer: it is grounded in Scripture. This is evident in the marvelous hymn of praise and thanksgiving which Mary left us as a treasured heritage.

When Mary and Elizabeth shared their awareness of God's miraculous workings in their lives, Mary's jubilant Magnificat revealed her intimate knowledge of the Scriptures. Much of this knowledge came from Mary's participation in the liturgy of her day—celebrating the Passover festivals in Jerusalem, for example, and praying the joyous hymns of praise and thanksgiving with her people as they worshiped in the temple. Mary's own song of praise thus draws from many biblical texts, as she recounts the wonderful deeds of God for his people down through the ages.

Mary's use and love of Scripture may have been what Jesus was alluding to when a woman in the crowd praised his mother for giving him birth and nurturing him. Jesus must have been pleased at these words, but perhaps he was gently pointing to Mary's true greatness when he responded, "Blessed rather are those who hear the word of God and keep it" (Lk 11:28). Mary not only heard the word of God: she knew it, prayed it, and let it be her guiding light.

Turn to the Bible!

Mary's knowledge and use of Scripture is an ideal to which the Holy Father calls us in his apostolic letter on the third millennium.

This is a directive of paramount importance for renewing our love for Jesus and deepening our relationship with him.

> In order to recognize who Christ truly is, Christians should turn with renewed interest to the Bible, whether it be through the liturgy, rich in the divine word, or through devotional reading, or through instructions suitable for the purpose and other aids.[1]

"Devotional reading" is also called praying with Scripture. In using Scripture as the basis of prayer, we select a word or short passage to bring us to a conscious awareness of the Lord's presence, his unconditional love and tender care of us. As his word finds a home in our heart, it will influence our thinking and attitudes, which in turn will mold and transform our actions. Spending time daily with the Lord's word will enable us to form the mind and heart of Christ within us.

In our times the Holy Spirit is drawing thousands of people to his word, especially as found in the Gospel. He is speaking to their hearts through it. Through our daily praying with Scripture he will speak to our hearts too. What better way to prepare for and contribute to the coming of the third millennium?

Contemplative Prayer

"In the coming age," theologian Karl Rahner once said, "we must all be mystics or be nothing at all." Mystical, or contemplative, prayer is indeed the goal of the "ever more intensive prayer" to which the Holy Spirit wishes to draw us as we approach the expected renewal of the millennium. By his gentle guidance and inspiration the Spirit is inviting and encouraging every one of us to become an active contemplative in the world.

Contemplative prayer is a powerful, in-depth prayer that leads us beyond words (vocal prayer) and beyond reflections about God (meditation) to the reality of God dwelling with us and within us. Ideally, all prayer should have this contemplative quality. Contemplation goes by many names: prayer of the heart, listening prayer, prayer of simplicity, prayer of awareness, wordless prayer. All of these express some important aspect of contemplation, but what it is defies definition since it is a deep, personal experience of God.

We are well aware that no words have been coined to describe adequately an interior experience of the heart. How much less can words define a contemplative experience of God! It is an awareness in the depth of our being that God knows and loves us with an unconditional love. When Jesus tells us, "Abide in my love" (Jn 15:9), he is directing us toward this prayer of contemplation. As we rest and bask alone in the hallowed sunshine of the Lord's love, we permit the words of Jesus to find a home in our heart: "As the Father has loved me, so I have loved you" (Jn 15:9).

Queen of Contemplatives

We have already seen how Mary's wordless listening prayer guided her in discerning God's perfect will for her life. As Mary pondered God's workings and sought to give herself exclusively to him, her prayer for the most part became a silent attentiveness.

One particular episode in Scripture which manifests Mary's contemplative prayer posture took place in the stark poverty of the cave in Bethlehem. When the shepherds arrived, they somehow grasped the great mystery which was taking place in their midst. They saw beyond the vulnerability and helplessness of the child and recognized something divine. "When they saw it, they made known the saying which had been told them concerning this child" (Lk 2:17).

The shepherds had been receptive to the angel's message; they had believed and had come to the cave. Their faith and obedience were rewarded, for now they understood. They left the cave glorifying and praising God.

It must have startled Mary not only that the shepherds came, but that to some extent they recognized her helpless, vulnerable babe as the promised Messiah. This was beyond Mary's human comprehension. When the shepherds left, Scripture tells us, Mary took this unusual happening to prayer, quietly reflecting on all that was taking place: "But Mary kept all these things, pondering them in her heart" (Lk 2:19).

This episode shows Mary as a real contemplative. Humanly speaking she did not understand, but she contemplated in her heart the mysterious workings of God and was moved to give herself with greater trust and love to his divine will.

Whether consciously or not, many artists have affirmed Mary's position as a true contemplative by the way they have portrayed her at the manger. This is even true of many designers of Christmas cards! Over the years I have enjoyed reviewing the greeting cards I have received at Christmas. I am deeply impressed as I discover how often Mary is pictured rapt in reverent awe and wonder as she gazes at her newborn Son. Whether she is kneeling or standing, her posture as well as her peaceful expression reveal a prayerful awareness of the divine displayed before her very eyes. She seems oblivious to everything else around her, alone with the Lord.

Learning to Pray

When Thomas Merton was asked to teach someone how to pray contemplatively, he informed the person that it would be easier to teach him how to become an angel! Contemplative prayer cannot be taught. It must be learned by experience. A spiritual director may assist us with prudent advice, but ultimately it is the grace of the Holy Spirit which draws us into this method of prayer. He does so only after we give ourselves totally to the influence of his grace.

Because contemplative prayer is a special gift of the Spirit, we must keep ourselves receptive and cooperative with his grace, asking him to pray within us. St. Paul reminds us that we must be attentive to the leading of the Holy Spirit if we are to pray well.

The Spirit helps us in our weakness; for we do not know how to pray as we ought, but the Spirit himself intercedes for us with sighs too deep for words. And he who searches the hearts of men knows what is the mind of the Spirit, because the Spirit intercedes for the saints according to the will of God.

ROMANS 8:26-27

If we ask him, the Holy Spirit will also lead us gently into that silence which is indispensable to contemplation. This he does when he bids us, "Be still, and know that I am God" (Ps 46:10), and again, "Be still before the Lord, and wait patiently for him" (Ps 37:7). Silence leads us into a peaceful, prayerful life here on earth and into the abundant life in heaven. Again the Holy Spirit urges us, "Incline your ear, and come to me; hear that your soul may live" (Is 55:3).

Prayer of Listening

We can cooperate with the Spirit's efforts to lead us into contemplation by doing what we can to pursue a twofold silence in our prayer life. We can maintain exterior silence, which means no communication, verbal or otherwise. And we can seek interior silence. This comes as we relax and quiet ourselves, setting aside all the mundane concerns, preoccupations, and distractions that fill our day.

The purpose of this silence, of course, is to free us to listen, to put our attention exclusively on the Lord. This type of single-minded attention is well illustrated by a "Family Circus" cartoon: it shows a father sitting in a comfortable chair reading a newspaper, while his little son tugs on his arm and says, "Daddy, listen to me with your eyes!"

God wants us to be aware of his presence, to listen to him with our whole being by putting ourselves totally before him. The Lord wants us to bring our emptiness to him that he may fill us with himself. In an article entitled "Simple Prayer,"[2] Carmelite Sister Wendy Mary Beckett offers this brief directive for entering into the prayer of listening: "The essential act of prayer is to stand unprotected before God. What will God do? He will take possession of us." Coming "unprotected before God" is an ideal way of listening with our heart to what he wishes to convey to us.

In time our prayer of listening will also become a prayer of awareness. Through it we will become profoundly aware of God's presence around us—in nature, in other people, in all the events of life, and, more importantly, within ourselves. As this interior awareness develops, we will delight to simply be alone in God's loving presence.

Images from Daily Life

As mentioned above, it is impossible to define this contemplative prayer of aloneness with the Lord. However a few images drawn from ordinary life may help us to understand it better.

Sun bath. Entering into prayer may be compared to taking a sun bath. We place ourselves in the sunshine and simply rest there, permitting the sun to warm and relax us. Just as we bask in the sunshine, permitting the sun to do its work, so we bask in the warmth of God's love and presence, allowing his love to mold and transform us.

Dry sponge. When we prepare our hearts for prayer by emptying ourselves of all our daily concerns in order to concentrate on the Lord, we are like a dry sponge. Dropped into the limitless ocean of God's love, we become saturated with his divine life and love.

Plowed field. When a field is plowed and prepared for planting, the soil is loose and porous. After it is seeded, it awaits a gentle rain so that the seed can germinate and eventually produce a good harvest. We prepare ourselves to be good soil by trying to be open and receptive to the Lord's presence; then we permit the living water of his grace and loving care to produce a harvest within us.

Magnificent sunset—or a beautiful flower, a towering mountain, the smile of a child. Any of the myriad works of God's creative love can stand as images pointing to the transformation that God wants to work in us. Although imperfect, the beauties of our world reflect something of God's own beauty and can draw us into prayer of praise and contemplation.

Prayer of the Heart

Contemplative prayer is also known as prayer of the heart. We need to experience God with our heart in order to love him.

A person may know very much about God but not know him as a personal, loving God. We may know God intellectually and theologically without ever having experienced him in our heart as a caring, concerned, loving Father who provides for us. Similarly, we may be familiar with the historical Jesus without really having experienced him as a personal God whose boundless love led him to the cross for our sake. We may never have realized that Jesus was addressing us personally when he said, "No one has greater love than this, to lay down one's life for one's friends" (Jn 15:13, NRSV)!

Praying with our heart is listening at the core of our being to what Jesus is telling us about himself. He will reveal himself and enable us to know him with that heart knowledge which enkindles and nurtures love.

"We cannot love a person we do not know, and we cannot know a person to whom we have not listened," says a time-tested axiom. This is true of God. We may know very much about the theology of God, but we cannot know him as a personal God until we have listened to him. Only then can we love him.

As we rest prayerfully, listening to the Lord at the depths of our being, the Holy Spirit penetrates our human ego with all its pre-occupations and distractions. He prays within our spirit, molding and transforming our thoughts and attitudes and enabling us to put on the mind and heart of Jesus. We listen with our heart and we are touched by love.

This prayer of the heart is experiencing God. Even though no thoughts fill our minds and no words are spoken, we are communing with the mystery of God, and our hearts are being transformed.

Fruits of Prayer

As we continue to pray contemplatively, we will enjoy many of the fruits this prayer produces within us. Here are just a few of them.

1. *Heartfelt motivation.* As we listen in the depths of our being to the Lord speaking to us, we will derive inspiration and motivation for our daily routine tasks, which might otherwise become monotonous drudgery.

2. *Heartfelt conversion.* A conversion of heart takes place within us even though we may not be aware of it with our minds. It can be painless. As we expose our attitudes and thinking to the

Lord, we will become aware of whether or not we are in tune with his mind and heart. If we are not, a conversion process begins to take place within our heart.

3. Heartfelt transformation. The conversion begun in our heart will eventually affect our whole being. In contemplative prayer, the Holy Spirit praying with us will mold and transform our lives. As we prayerfully listen deep within our hearts, we will be putting on the mind and heart of the Lord.

4. Heartfelt response to the Lord. Perhaps the most important fruit of contemplation is the fact that we will come to know the Lord with our heart and not merely with our head. We will be quicker to grasp what Jesus says about himself in the Gospel—for example, in "I AM" passages like, "I am the light of the world" (Jn 8:12) and, "I am the way, and the truth, and the life" (Jn 14:6). We will also be more attuned to Jesus as he reveals his heart by his attitudes and actions toward the poor, the downtrodden, the sick. "Learn from me, for I am gentle and lowly in heart," Jesus says (Mt 11:29)—and we will respond from the heart.

5. Heartfelt compassion. Contemplative prayer conditions us to bring the Lord's love, peace, and joy to a suffering world. Through our own transformation, we bring healing and compassion to the bruised and battered Body of Christ in the world. We fulfill our calling to be Christ-bearers—to be the presence of Christ everywhere we go.

Contemplation: Path to a "New Self"

Fundamentally, the fruit of contemplation has to do with forming the image of Jesus in us. St. Paul reminds us that this image was planted within us at the time of our Baptism: "As many of you as were baptized into Christ have put on Christ" (Gal 3:27). St. Paul entreats us to "put on the Lord Jesus Christ" (Rom 13:14), to fulfill our mission in life by growing and maturing in radiating the image of Jesus. Again Paul urges:

> You were taught to put away your former way of life... and to be renewed in the spirit of your minds, and to clothe yourselves with the new self, created according to the likeness of God in true righteousness and holiness. EPHESIANS 4:22-24, NRSV

Putting on the "new self" is an ongoing process which must be supported and developed by a life of contemplative prayer. Keeping our focus always on the Lord will help us to enter into contemplative prayer and be more receptive to its transforming power. St. Paul assures us:

> All of us, with unveiled faces, seeing the glory of the Lord as though reflected in a mirror, are being transformed into the same image from one degree of glory to another; for this comes from the Lord, the Spirit. 2 CORINTHIANS 3:18, NRSV

We become what we contemplate. As we gaze on the Lord in prayer, we will gradually become more and more like him—a divine gift which is not simply for ourselves. By our attitudes and actions we are to reflect the mind and heart of Christ to everyone we encounter along the pathway of life. With its transforming ability to enable us to see others as God sees them, to love others with his heart, to serve others as Jesus served, contemplation will make this goal possible for us.

Unique Privilege, Unique Partner

Try to fathom for a moment what is taking place when we try to pray contemplatively. The transcendent God of heaven and earth, the God of power and might, the Lord of all the angels and saints, the Creator and Energizer of the whole universe wants to communicate with us—with each one of us, personally and individually. Nothing else in all the world should matter at that time! God wants to be with us, and in prayer he wants us to be exclusively for him.

Mary stands as a sign of God's great desire to be with us through prayer. Given to us as our model and exemplar, her lifestyle guides us into a life of committed prayer. As our companion in prayer, Mary leads us to Jesus, inspiring and motivating us to commune with God in the very depths of our being and to open our hearts wide to receive the unbounded influx of divine love.

NINE

MARY: MODEL OF FAITH AND HOPE
The Early Life and Ministry of Jesus

"This is the victory that overcomes the world, our faith."
1 JOHN 5:4

"'Tis not the dying for a faith that's so hard,
'tis the living up to it that's difficult."
WILLIAM M. THACKERAY

Our society today is experiencing a major crisis of faith. In this computer age we have made such vast strides in technology that we have become a self-sufficient, sophisticated people. God has become irrelevant in the lives of many people, who put their faith instead in their own ingenuity. Inundated with hedonistic culture, some find God's moral standards too restrictive, depriving them of their supposed freedom. Other people are so engrossed in a struggle for success, power, and wealth that they have little time even to think about God.

Counteracting this waning faith is one of the desired expectations of the next millennium, as specified in Pope John Paul II's apostolic letter "The Coming of the Third Millennium." The Pope challenges us to return to a vibrant, dynamic faith in God and in one another:

Everything ought to focus on the primary objective of the Jubilee: the strengthening of faith and of the witness of Christians.[1]

In these troubled times God's special emissary, his Mother, is pleading with us to strive earnestly for a strong, dynamic, operative faith. As we have seen, she is doing this through her apparitions—the extraordinary means that God resorts to in times of crisis to arrest our attention and challenge us to return to his way of life. In all Mary's messages throughout the second millennium, faith and hope in God are the central themes, whether expressed or implied.

But Mary's very life also gives a powerful teaching about these virtues, for they characterized Mary's entire sojourn on earth. In this chapter, we will focus on how Mary's undaunted faith and hope illumined the period of her life between Jesus' birth and death. Like a flashlight, Mary's example guides us along the path we are to follow in the present-day crisis in faith.

What Do We Mean by Faith?

Faith is a firm belief in God and in all the divine truths he has revealed. It is an implicit trust in his loving providence overshadowing us at all times. Faith is the firm conviction that God loves us with an unconditional, immutable love, regardless of who we are or what we may have done.

Scripture says: "Faith is the assurance of things hoped for, the conviction of things not seen," and then cautions us: "Without faith it is impossible to please him" (Heb 11:1, 6). Faith is thus the foundation of our spiritual life and is basic to our relationship with the Lord.

Faith is a gift from God that is implanted in us as a tiny seed and nurtured by the Holy Spirit's presence within us. However,

God does not force his divine gifts upon us. He offers them and waits for us to accept and use them.

As we step out in faith at all times and in all circumstances, our own faith will increase and mature. As we exercise this gift of faith the Holy Spirit will strengthen and build our confidence and trust in God, which in turn will bring us much peace and joy.

Levels of Faith

Our maturing faith normally progresses through different levels.

Intellectual assent to a truth which we cannot fully understand is the first level of faith. This happens when we decide to believe a fact which is presented with a sufficient amount of evidence to warrant our accepting it as credible. Here we are speaking about faith in spiritual truths. This differs from natural faith, which all human beings exercise in order to live each day. For example, I do not fully understand how electricity works, but I have faith that when I turn on a switch, the light will come on.

Faith in spiritual truth is different. For example, the mystery of the Holy Trinity is revealed in Scripture, but it is beyond our comprehension. When we give credence to it, our faith is on the level of intellectual assent. To paraphrase St. Thomas Aquinas: "I do believe, Lord. So what if I don't understand!"

Faith of commitment, the second stage of faith, enables us to commit our lives to some special vocation, calling, project, or program. Every good marriage is based on the faith of commitment, as is also the religious life.

A faith commitment can also be temporary. A person entering the religious life makes temporary vows for some time before making final or solemn vows. A person who believes in a particular project or program and is willing to pledge their time and talent for a definite period is making a temporary commitment, even though his or her faith in the program continues unabated. One such example would be a person who thoroughly believes in spreading the gospel of the Lord in foreign lands, but can give only a certain amount of time toward that effort.

Faith of expectancy is the next level to which we progress. With this degree of faith we confidently feel, know, believe, and trust that God does act in every situation in our lives. We know that he cares for us, that his love is so extravagant that everything that happens to us is for our good. This is the level of faith to which we are all called. As we pray with faith and trust, as we confidently accept God as the center and priority in our lives, we will then live with this expectant faith which is most pleasing to God.

Paragon of Faith

God not only permitted his Mother to appear in order to caution us of the crisis of faith in the world and to encourage us to live a more committed life of faith; he also gave his Mother to us as our ideal, a perfect model of extraordinary faith.

Mary was a paragon of faith throughout her whole life—from the time she first appeared in salvation history at the Annunciation until the last mention of her in the Upper Room, where she had assembled with the apostles to pray fervently for the outpouring of the Holy Spirit after the Ascension. With Mary at our side, then, let us relive not her whole life but rather those episodes that took place during the early life and ministry of Jesus. As we do, we will see that this was a time which called Mary to particularly great faith, trust, and hope in God.

Presentation in the Temple

Mary's faith—tested at the Annunciation, praised by Elizabeth at the Visitation, and tested again by the arduous journey to Bethlehem—must have been severely tried on various occasions immediately after Jesus' birth.

Like all devout Jewish parents of the day, Mary and Joseph brought their newborn Son to the temple in Jerusalem "to present him to the Lord, as it is written in the law of the Lord" (see Lk 2:22-38). But the peaceful joy of being able to offer Jesus to the Father in the magnificent temple was suddenly interrupted by the prophecy of Simeon:

> This child is destined for the falling and rising of many in Israel, and a sign that will be opposed... and a sword will pierce your own soul too. LUKE 2:34, NRSV

What must have gone through Mary's mind as she heard the puzzling, portentous words of this devout old man? What did she think of his joyful prayer of resignation: "Master, now you are dismissing your servant in peace..."? Did it startle Mary to see her Son so clearly recognized as the Messiah by both Simeon and the prophetess Anna?

Whatever understanding Mary may have had of Jesus' coming mission, it was clearly incomplete at that time: "And his father and mother marvelled at what was said about him" (Lk 2:33). Only a Mother with great faith and hope could peacefully hold such statements in her heart, while trusting God to unfold their meaning in his own time.

Egyptian Exile

Mary's faith must also have been put to the test when it became clear that she and her family would have to flee into Egypt to escape Herod's murderous attempt to eliminate her Son. But Mary believed that the words of the angel to Joseph were guidance from God:

> Rise, take the child and his mother, and flee to Egypt, and remain there till I tell you; for Herod is about to search for the child, to destroy him.   MATTHEW 2:13

Mary could have resisted and protested, "Why, Lord?" She could have grumbled about being denied the joy of sharing the birth of her first-born child with her family and friends. But instead, Mary's faith prompted her to set out immediately and wholeheartedly on that weary journey into a strange country. Though Scripture is silent on the topic, we may suppose that Mary's faith also sustained her through the trials of living among strangers in a foreign land.

Lost in the Temple

Another episode when Mary might have questioned God's ways occurred when her Son was lost for three days (see Lk 2:41-52). The Holy Family had gone to Jerusalem for the feast of the Passover, as they did each year. Perhaps this year had been the occasion of Jesus' bar mitzvah, since he was now twelve and considered an adult. On their way home, Mary and Joseph suddenly realized that they had lost their son.

Like any good mother, Mary was anxious about her son's welfare (she said so herself: see Lk 2:48). Many questions and concerns must have flooded Mary's mind as she searched.

What joy and relief when she and Joseph finally found Jesus in the temple, "sitting among the teachers, listening to them and asking them questions" (Lk 2:46). And it must have been an added joy to hear Jesus speaking so intelligently that "all who heard him were amazed at his understanding and his answers" (Lk 2:47).

Still, the reasons for Jesus' disappearance were somewhat puzzling. So was his reply to his parents' anxiety: "How is it that you sought me? Did you not know that I must be in my Father's house?" (Lk 2:49). Mary did not quite understand. But again she responded with faith, accepting this painful experience as part of God's inscrutable plan and pondering it in her heart (see Lk 2:51).

The Hidden Life at Nazareth

Scripture is virtually silent about the eighteen or so years between the finding of Jesus in the temple and the beginning of his public ministry. This period is summarized in two verses:

> And he went down with them and came to Nazareth, and was obedient to them.... And Jesus increased in wisdom and in stature, and in favor with God and man.   LUKE 2:51, 52

Without knowing the particulars, however, one thing we may confidently assume is that the home in Nazareth was a house of prayer and a haven of faith. The Holy Family must have often prayed together as they meditated on the mysterious plan of God unfolding in their lives. In that quiet home there must have been long periods of reflective silence. Jesus' spiritual growth in his human nature was the fruit of the long hours of prayer he spent alone with his Father, but also the times he prayed with Mary and Joseph.

There are many lessons for us here. The Lord intends our own homes to be a vestibule of heaven. The Second Vatican Council speaks of our homes as a domestic church. As we heed Mary's example of faith-filled prayer and implore her powerful interces- sion, our home and family will be protected against the ravages of our pagan culture.

Family Prayer of Faith

Father Patrick Peyton, the tireless promoter of the Rosary Crusade, used to maintain adamantly that "the family that prays together stays together."

The truth of this statement is confirmed by some facts pub- lished by the United States Bureau of Statistics. According to this study, one out of every two marriages in our country will end in divorce. However, among couples who are married in a church and who continue to attend church, statistics show that only one out of fifty marriages dissolve. The next statistic is even more encouraging: The divorce rate among couples who are married in a church, continue to worship in a church, and are faithful in pray- ing as a family is only one out of 1105 marriages.

A family's example of Christian living, strengthened by prayer, will be a witness to other families and draw them closer to the Lord. Eventually their influence will reach out far and wide. Thus, as a family goes, so goes our society. Only when Christian values of harmony, honesty, integrity, and love of God and neighbor are taught and practiced in our homes will our society be turned toward God.

Faith-filled prayer is the sure path to the great Christian revital- ization we eagerly anticipate in the coming millennium. Jesus reas- sures us of the effectiveness of such prayer, promising that it will be heard and answered: "For everyone who asks receives; and he who seeks, finds; and to him who knocks it will be opened" (Lk 11:10).

As the Holy Family prayed together in faith for the unfolding of God's plan, today's families can pray together in faith for the fruits of the millennium. And Jesus promises results!

Again I say to you, if two of you agree on earth about anything they ask, it will be done for them by my Father in heaven. For where two or three are gathered in my name, there am I in the midst of them. MATTHEW 18:19-20

Farewell to Nazareth

The years had flown by so quickly. Now the peaceful solitude of Nazareth was drawing to a painful close. According to the Father's plan, Jesus must now begin his public ministry by proclaiming the Good News of salvation to all people. Mary knew that, according to the prophecies, his teaching would lead him into persecution, rejection, suffering, and eventually his death on the cross.

What faith it must have demanded of Mary to offer Jesus to the world in this way! We can scarcely imagine the anguish generated in her heart when Jesus emerged from the cloistered peace and serenity of his home in Nazareth to begin his salvific mission. Mary's sorrow was intensified by her knowledge that her son would be rejected by his own people and his ministry would end in a cruel death as a common criminal.

Even though her pain was severe, Mary once again offered her son with faith and trust in the Father's loving plan. In her suffering she must have experienced moments of real peace, realizing that she had fulfilled her mission and was now giving Jesus to the people he loved.

Wedding Feast at Cana

Though we only catch occasional glimpses of Mary during Jesus' public ministry, she must have followed every step as closely as she could. Her most extensive appearance is at the wedding feast in Cana (see Jn 2:1-11).

Noticing that the wine was running low, Mary revealed her undaunted faith in her Son's power and loving care and concern for everyone's needs. When she told Jesus that the wine was failing, his answer seemed to manifest some indifference: "My hour has not yet come" (Jn 2:4). Yet Mary believed so firmly in her son's compassion and power that she said to the servers, "Do whatever he tells you" (Jn 2:5). Then, as the poet Richard Crashaw so expressively put it, "The conscious water saw its God and blushed."

Mary's firm faith not only initiated Jesus' first miracle, but it also sparked faith in the hearts of his disciples. As John says: "This, the first of his signs, Jesus did at Cana in Galilee, and manifested his glory; and his disciples believed in him" (Jn 2:11).

Mary's faith can also enkindle our own, if we too heed her gentle but persuasive admonition to "do whatever he tells you." Only because the servers at the wedding did what Jesus told them and filled the jars with water (and did it without understanding why!) was the whole wedding party able to enjoy unexpectedly delectable wine.

Similarly, only as we follow our Mother's directive to obey Jesus in faith will we see his grace transform the mediocrity of our lives into the sparkling wine of conversion and commitment.

Faith and Hope Go Hand in Hand

Closely related to faith and underlying all the episodes of Mary's life that we have mentioned is the virtue of hope. As Belgian Cardinal Godfried Danneels observed: "Isn't hope simply faith that is young and refuses to grow old?" The interrelatedness of these two virtues can be seen in this definition of hope from the *Catechism of the Catholic Church*:

> Hope is the theological virtue by which we desire the kingdom of heaven and eternal life as our happiness, placing our trust in Christ's promises and relying not on our own strength, but on the help of the grace of the Holy Spirit.[2]

When the Holy Spirit comes to dwell within us at the time of our Baptism, he implants within us the virtue of hope as a tiny seed. Throughout our life, he continues to give us all the help we need for this seed to develop and mature into a firm hope and an unflinching trust in God's loving care and fidelity.

Hope has two dimensions. In the first place, it strengthens our trust and confidence in the midst of all the trials and tribulations, as well as all the joys and blessings of life. Second, it engenders a longing within us to be united with God for all eternity, realizing that our loving Father will help us to attain our eternal destiny.

As the *Catechism* says: "By hope we desire, and with steadfast trust await from God, eternal life and the graces to merit it."[3] Our hope also includes the desire that all people will come to the Lord and enjoy eternal happiness.

With Hope Undaunted

Even though the biographical data about Mary is very sparse, her life does reflect all the aspects of genuine Christian hope. Her example might well serve to illustrate St. Paul's admonition to us: "Rejoice in your hope, be patient in tribulation, be constant in prayer" (Rom 12:12).

Contemplating Mary's way of life will strengthen and develop our own gift of hope. Mary's strong hope in the face of the many trials and difficulties she had to endure sets a course for us to follow. Without a doubt Mary would endorse St. Peter's advice: "Cast all your anxieties on him, for he cares about you." (1 Pt 5:7).

There were many occasions when Mary had to cast all her anxieties on the Lord. She did this with the awareness, born of hope, that God cares for us and will bring only good out of his mysterious plans.

Mary's confident trust and firm hope prevailed and sustained her when the Holy Family secretly stole out of Bethlehem at night to escape the murderous designs of Herod. Mary cast all her anxieties on the Lord when the boy Jesus disappeared at the Passover festival. Later her undaunted hope would support her when she stood at the praetorium and heard her son condemned to death as a common criminal. Hope kept her standing at the cross to witness the outpouring of Jesus' redemptive love. Mary placed her hope in God, who "so loved the world that he gave his only Son, that whoever believes in him should not perish but have eternal life" (Jn 3:16).

Indeed, so strong is Mary's example of hope that the Second Vatican Council calls Mary "the sign of created hope and solace to the wandering people of God." The same Council document, *Lumen Gentium* ("The Dogmatic Constitution on the Church"), even declares Mary to be the image of the Church, since both are the source of our hope:

In the interim just as the Mother of Jesus, glorified in body and soul in heaven, is the image and beginning of the Church as it is to be perfected in the world to come, so too does she shine forth on earth, until the day of the Lord shall come, as a sign of sure hope and solace to the people of God during its sojourn on earth.[4]

Mother of Hope

As the Church believes, so she prays—thus the many prayers by which Catholics implore Mary's intercession as the Mother of hope. Among the many Masses that honor Mary and seek her maternal help is one that honors her as the Mother of Divine Hope. This Mass venerates Mary because in her life on earth she steadfastly practiced the virtue of hope, and because she is the beacon of hope for all of us on our pilgrimage heavenward.

In our personal prayers we often place our hope in Mary's powerful intercession. Whenever we pray the Memorare, we ask her to

Remember, O most gracious Virgin Mary, that never was it known that anyone who fled to your protection, implored your help, or sought your intercession was left unaided.

Our hope in eternal salvation is strengthened every time we ask our Mother Mary to "pray for us sinners now and at the hour of our death."

As the most loving Mother of them all, Mary is always ready to intercede for us, because she wants only the best for her children. Her heart's desire for us is expressed in the prayer of St. Paul: "May the God of hope fill you with all joy and peace in believing, so that by the power of the Holy Spirit you may abound in hope" (Rom 15:13).

Beacon of Hope

How urgently we need to develop an expectant, trusting hope as we enter into the Great Renewal and revitalization of our Christian way of life in this third millennium. Hope gives us the assurance of the Holy Spirit's love which is being poured into the heart of every person who is receptive to his gift of divine life and love. Our fervent hope assures us that by his power and loving concern the Spirit will guide and support us along the way, as we strive to fulfill our personal role in the Great Millennial Renewal.

And so during these preparation days Pope John Paul invites us to contemplate Mary, our Mother, as "a woman of hope who, like Abraham, accepted God's will 'hoping against hope'" (Rom 4:18). As the Pope's letter goes on to point out, Mary is "a radiant model for those who entrust themselves with all their hearts to the promises of God."[5]

Our Call to Faith and Hope

"The Coming of the Third Millennium" also reminds us that our primary objective for the Jubilee must be to strengthen our own faith and become a witness to others. This calling may seem like a formidable undertaking. But with the guidance of the Holy Spirit and the powerful intercession of Mary, the woman of faith and hope, we can launch out on our mission with the assurance that we will succeed, to the extent that the Lord has determined.

Each one of us has a tremendous potential and power to counteract the decline in faith so rampant around us. Each one of us can bring hope into situations that are marked by discouragement and despair. We have only to turn to God and trust in his word. Dynamic, fervent faith and hope will solve many of the problems facing us today and help us avoid many of the tragic happenings in our country and the world.

At this juncture, we may be tempted to object: "I am only one person in this whole wide world! What influence do I have, or how much impact can I have on others?"

If we live with a strong, vibrant faith and hope, our whole lifestyle will reflect our deep trust and confidence in God. Without our even being aware of it, we will radiate our attitudes. People around us will begin to put their faith in God, to believe that God has a future and a hope for them.

If you influence just one person each month, and if that person in turn then influences one other person each month, do you know how many people you will touch annually? Four thousand! Yes, you can make a difference!

The Holy Spirit assures us: "This is the victory that conquers the world, our faith" (1 Jn 5:4). As we earnestly strive, with faith and hope, to emulate Mary's example and heed her maternal advice, we will be on the road to that promised victory. She whose faith and hope never wavered will help us to see that God's ways are not our ways and that God brings only good out of everything he asks us to accept.

TEN

MARY: MODEL OF SUFFERING
The Passion and Death of Christ

"Standing near the cross of Jesus was his Mother."
JOHN 19:25, NRSV

"Where there is sorrow there is holy ground."
DE PROFUNDIS

Suffering, pain, and sorrow, so much a part of our human condition, remain a tantalizing, baffling, unsolved mystery. Not even the greatest minds throughout the ages have succeeded in finding the key to a plausible explanation. What people of faith know, however, is that God never permits anything to happen to us without a definite purpose. St. Augustine is among those who assure us that nothing besets us in life from which God cannot bring some good.

Affliction of any kind can be a powerful means of conditioning us to enter into a closer union with the Lord. Every pain or sorrow can raise us to a higher level of receptivity to what the Lord wants to work within us. In some mysterious way, suffering—be it mental anguish, physical pain, or spiritual suffering—can sanctify us, since it gives the Lord an opportunity to transform and mold our minds and hearts. It also helps us to better reflect the mind and heart of Jesus to everyone we meet.

Our Lady of Sorrows

Mary was not spared from walking the rocky road of suffering and pain. She was not exempt from the hardships and heartaches which are the normal lot of humanity.

One of Mary's greater sorrows was the rejection which Jesus received from the people he had come to save. This is one of the reasons why Mary is anxious to be the guiding Star for us in these days of millennial renewal. She does not want us, his people, to reject her son and the way of life he mapped out for us.

As she patiently and willingly endured her lot in life, Mary is our model and our Mother of Sorrows. Her fervent prayer is that we accept all the distress which comes into our life as the path which leads to our sanctification.

Mary, our Mother, is a perfect model and exemplar in any phase of suffering we may be enduring. Mary knows what it means to suffer: her deep suffering, united with that of her Son, fulfilled an important role in the redemption of the human race.

Mary also assures us that she will be our comforting companion every step of the way on our journey heavenward. In his dying moments, amid agonizing pain, Jesus gave us his Mother to be a model and comfort in whatever affliction may assail us. When pain, suffering, and hardships come our way, we can therefore be certain that our caring Mother will be there to comfort and accompany us through every pain.

The World's Most Gripping Short Story

About the turn of the century Will Porter began his journalistic career by writing short stories under the pen name of O. Henry. He was a prolific and popular writer of nearly three hundred short stories.

O. Henry had a flair for building up suspense in the ordinary events of life. He was in touch with human nature and saw humor and pathos in all life's experiences.

Many centuries before O. Henry's creative writings were published, St. John the Evangelist wrote a short story that has deeply touched the hearts of millions of people throughout the world. John developed his story without one adjective or adverb, yet what pathos in his brief account of only one sentence.

> Standing near the cross of Jesus were his mother and his mother's sister, Mary, the wife of Clopas and Mary of Magdala.
>
> JOHN 19:25, NRSV

This short, short story recorded by John reveals and emphasizes one of the specific roles which Mary was asked to fulfill in God's plan for our salvation. It is commemorated on the feast of Our Lady of Sorrows, celebrated on September 15, when we remember that Mary accepted all the suffering, from the crib to the cross, that her mission in life entailed. Her sinlessness gave her a deeper insight into the gravity of the rejection of her son as the Messiah by her own people, whom he had come to save. Her deep disappointment caused her much heartache. Her suffering was intensified when she heard Jesus condemned as a common criminal, and saw him crucified beyond the walls of the Holy City, by which his enemies intended to bring him even greater disgrace.

Mary is appropriately called Our Lady of Sorrows, and Mother of Sorrows.

Preparation for Calvary

The scene on Calvary is the climax of Mary's suffering—and the episode of her life on which this chapter will focus. But that oblation was prepared by many episodes of suffering and surrender. Though we have already looked at these other events of

Mary's life, let us examine them again briefly in the light of what they reveal of her experience of pain and sorrow.

Problems of pregnancy. On her return to Nazareth after her joyful visit with Elizabeth in Ain Karim, Mary was deeply pained because Joseph could not understand her pregnancy. Remember that, according to the customs of the day, Joseph could not accept Mary as his wife in that condition. He agonized over the situation.

We can well imagine the terrible suffering Mary went through because she was suspected by Joseph—suffering that came to an end only when God sent his angel to reassure Joseph. God permitted this suffering in the lives of these two precious people because he wanted to strengthen their faith and trust in his divine designs.

God permits misunderstandings and strained relationships mingled with doubts and fears to show us our human weakness and our need to place implicit trust in him. As our trust in God increases, our trust in others will also deepen. Every problem, pain, difficulty, or hardship that comes our way will be beneficial for our spiritual maturation.

Journey to Bethlehem. When Mary went with Joseph to obey the decree of the Roman government "that all the world should be registered," she left family and friends behind in Nazareth. Family ties were very strong, which discouraged travel, and traveling was arduous. This separation must have been difficult for Mary, causing her loneliness and pain. Her suffering was also intensified by her physical condition and the uncertainty of the time for her delivery.

The Lord speaks to us through many and various channels, even through secular authority and customs. As law-abiding citizens, we too might find certain restrictions and regulations curtailing our freedom to do what we would otherwise prefer. This sacrifice can be painful also. As I write this I think of a Vietnamese immigrant with whom I am closely associated. He is now a citizen of the United States, and has been waiting several years for his wife to join him in this country because of U.S. immigration laws. The fact that he is a hardworking person who is able to provide for their subsistence adds to the heartache.

There are several aspects of the life of the Holy Family, too, that model for us the necessity of suffering and surrender.

No room in the inn. The birthing room for the Lord of heaven and earth was a stark, cold cave on a hillside in the shepherds' field. The exuberant joy of the coming of the Savior of the world was somewhat dimmed by the lack of the comforts and conveniences of home. As poor pilgrims this was all Mary and Joseph could offer the newborn King of the Jews.

No doubt Mary regretted her inability to offer her son more of the amenities of life. This disappointment must have caused her pain. Her uncomplaining acceptance speaks to us.

When our limited means cannot supply all the comforts and conveniences we desire in life, Mary's quiet attitude of acceptance and adjustment will enable us to resign ourselves and enjoy the many blessings we have. Our gracious Father knows that some of the things we desire may not be conducive to our salvation and may lead us further from him. Mary will help us utter our "fiat."

Sword of sorrow. How stricken Mary must have felt to hear Simeon's prophecy that her child would be "a sign that is spoken against" and that her own soul would be pierced by a sword (Lk 2:34-35).

Like all faithful Jews, Mary had waited and longed for the coming of the Messiah who would redeem the world. Suddenly Mary hears the awful words that Jesus will not be accepted as the Messiah, but will be rejected and persecuted, a sign of contradiction. The sword of sorrow was already piercing her maternal heart.

Exile in Egypt. Jesus had barely come into the world when the rejections began. The words of the angel to Joseph, directing him to flee, penetrated deeply and painfully into Mary's heart. The flight to Egypt caused Mary's motherly heart another piercing sorrow of separation. In order to save her son from a cruel death, Mary had to renounce the joy of living with family and friends.

It was not only the exile, but the reason for it that caused Mary pain: Herod was seeking to destroy her child, who had come into the world as its Savior. Jesus came to bring salvation to her people and to the world, and even at this early stage he was persecuted. Imagine the depth of agony and pain of this sinless Mother at this threat to the very life of her infant son.

There could be another dimension to the suffering which Mary experienced. As the Holy Family stole away from Bethlehem at night, Mary might have heard the weeping and wailing of the mothers whose sons were being torn from their arms and being slaughtered by the cruel soldiers of Herod. If Mary did not actually hear the plaintive cries of these mothers, she must have heard about them in her exile. The awareness that these innocent children were suffering martyrdom because of her son must have brought another pang of pain to Mary's heart.

Lost and found. Losing Jesus in the temple at the Passover when he was twelve years old must have been a time of great suffering for Mary. Perhaps she blamed herself for negligence. Perhaps she wondered if she would ever find Jesus again.

After all, Mary did not know that this loss was going to be temporary. Recalling Herod's desperate attempt to eliminate Jesus, Mary must have wondered whether some cruel fate had befallen her son. Had he been kidnapped? injured? Was he ill? Was he beginning his redemptive ministry? How Mary must have worried as she searched for Jesus.

Who of us can fathom Mary's painful concern? We must constantly remind ourselves that though Mary was sinless, she was perfectly human, with all the emotions and feelings which any one of us might experience. Mary's sinlessness made her suffering all the more severe, since her delicate soul was more deeply touched by these experiences.

Sad farewells. We have already seen how faith sustained Mary through the difficult time when Jesus left home to begin his public ministry. Let us now try to imagine how very great Mary's suffering must have been at having to let her son go.

Be present with Jesus and Mary in that simple home at Nazareth as those last days of peace and quiet are drawing rapidly to a close. As the day of Jesus' departure approaches, the periods of silence grow longer and longer. Few words are spoken, yet silence speaks eloquently what is in the hearts of mother and son.

Walk with Mary as she accompanies Jesus to the edge of the town. Be at her side as she watches Jesus eventually disappear on the distant horizon as he makes his way down to the Jordan River. Try to experience the void in Mary's heart and the emptiness in that humble home at Nazareth.

Perhaps this parting scene was too sacred for the Gospel writers to record. Some experiences in life cannot be put into words. Scripture tells us only: "In those days Jesus came from Nazareth of Galilee and was baptized by John in the Jordan" (Mk 1:9).

Rest prayerfully with this scene and try to imagine what your own feelings would be if Jesus walked out of your life. What could fill the void, the emptiness, the loss of a sense of direction, and above all the loss of the warmth of his love enveloping you? What would life be like without the Eucharist, without his mysterious presence within you? We would experience a painful void, yet our pain could not be compared with the ache in Mary's heart.

Good parents are often afflicted with an empty-nest syndrome as their fledglings leave home to make a life for themselves. Mary understands their loneliness and desires to bring them solace and help fill the emptiness they feel.

Jesus' public life. Though she remains in the background during this period, we can imagine Mary's keen interest in all of Jesus' activities. How she must have wondered about the care Jesus was receiving! How she must have longed to defend him when he was criticized, ridiculed, persecuted by his enemies! That too was denied Mary. She had said her "yes" to the Father and never once reneged on that "fiat."

We may experience a slightly similar situation whenever the Lord seems especially distant from us. Mary understands, and her intercession is most powerful.

Standing by the Cross

The suffering and sorrow which Mary experienced throughout her earthly life reached a climax on Calvary's hill. As her Son was struggling and gasping for breath in the throes of death by suffocation, Mary could only stand "near the cross of Jesus." How deeply that pain of separation cut into her heart. She could not reach Jesus' face to wipe away the dirt, blood, and spittle. His outstretched arms nailed to the cross could not embrace her, nor could she clasp him in her arms as his life slipped away. She could not whisper her love into Jesus' ear—so raucous were the insults, derision, and mockery leveled against him by his enemies.

Note well Mary's reaction. She did not play the role of a martyr. She did not threaten the executioners, or his enemies. She did not swoon with grief. She did not scream vengeance at the injustice which was being done to her innocent Son. No, Mary STOOD!

Mary was able to stand because, with her son, she had made her oblation to the Father for the salvation of mankind. By the total, unreserved gift of himself in love to the Father, Jesus made up for that tremendous lack of love that God's creatures failed to give. His YES to the Father was offered to compensate for the widespread refusal to love, which is to sin. Like Jesus and with him, Mary was always YES to the Father (see 2 Cor 1:19)—and, most notably, at the cross.

The cruel, inhuman torture of Jesus on Calvary fills us with sorrow and contrition. At the same time, as we gaze at Mary standing quietly at the foot of the cross, we are filled with quiet joy and deep gratitude. Her posture of peace and strength speaks of a willing sacrifice and reminds us that Jesus' redemptive death assures us of our eternal salvation.

Our Daily Cross

Jesus knew that suffering and pain would be our lot here during our earthly sojourn. He also realized that with our limited vision, we would not comprehend the mystery of suffering, even though much of our suffering is caused by man's inhumanity to man and also by our own self-centeredness. To comfort and console us, to aid and encourage us in our plight of suffering, Jesus gave us his Mother as our very own. From the cross Jesus bequeathed the precious gift of his Mother to us: "Behold, your Mother" (Jn 19:27).

Jesus himself remains with us as our comforter and consoler in life, but he wanted us to have a Mother, a person like ourselves, to be at our side to encourage and support us in our struggles when sorrow strikes. Jesus was aware that we would need a model and an exemplar for our journey heavenward. He knew we would need the love, care, and concern of a spiritual Mother who would be ever solicitous about us.

A Mother's Healing Love

From our own personal experience most of us know the healing touch of a mother's love. Mothers can kiss away hurt and pain, imagined or real.

Mary is our sorrowful Mother and she is also our healer. Having herself endured unimaginable pain, she understands our suffering, hardships, and frustrations. She is eager to bring us comfort and reassurance, if we implore her powerful intercession. Since Mary suffered so dreadfully herself, she can be and is most empathetic when we are hurting.

A mother cannot comfort a hurting child if the child does not come to her. If we take our pain to Mary in prayer, she will soothe our suffering and bring it to Jesus, that he may sanctify it and thus assuage our distress by giving it meaning and purpose. How powerfully Mary carries on her healing mission! Much of it goes unseen—but at Lourdes, to name only one obvious example of Mary's power, it has continued for over a hundred years.

As our Mother of Sorrows, our model and exemplar, Mary, through her powerful intercession, obtains for us strength and courage, comfort, and consolation, and ultimately peace and joy in times of sorrow and suffering. This is what Jesus intended when he said, "Behold, your Mother."

Mary, Our Comfort in Trials

It is entirely in the realm of possibility that we will have special need of Mary's intercession as we prepare for the third millennium. As we strive wholeheartedly to follow the recommendations for the coming renewal, we will no doubt experience various kinds of suffering to bring to Our Lady of Sorrows.

- It will require some discipline to devote time regularly to "ever more intense prayer."

- It may be necessary for us to forego some legitimate pleasure or relaxation in order to establish "a solidarity with one's neighbor, especially the most needy."

- We may experience some ridicule for not compromising on a principle.

- It is likely that we may incur some criticism or misunderstanding or be accused of having a "holier than thou" attitude as we strive to reflect the mind and heart of Jesus. We may be shunned even by our friends.

- We may even be persecuted by those who do not understand. This should be no surprise, for Jesus prepared us for this when he said, "If they persecuted me, they will persecute you" (Jn 15:20). How comforting and encouraging are the words of Jesus at such times: "Blessed are those who are persecuted for righteousness' sake, for theirs is the kingdom of heaven" (Mt 5:10).

- We may become frustrated and discouraged at our faltering efforts and lack of success in the process of pursuing the millennial goals of the "strengthening of our faith," the building of "a true longing for holiness" and "deep desire for conversion," and attaining a genuine "personal renewal."[1]

Come to Mary

Jesus was well aware of the difficulties we would encounter along the way, when he urged us to take up our cross daily and follow him. In facing heartaches and hardships, problems and pains, sorrow and suffering, Jesus would have us call to mind his Mother standing near the cross on Calvary. He would tell us, "Here is your Mother, who will be your inspiration and motivation, your comfort and support in all your trials and tribulations."

When our pathway in life is beset with the pain of separation and detachment, emptiness and loneliness, disappointments and discouragement, frustration and failure, we can pour out our heart to Mary, our Mother of Sorrows. She will understand, take us by the hand, and lead us to Jesus. There we will receive comfort and compassion, healing and love which will transform our pain into peaceful acceptance. All of this will better prepare us for the reconciliation and renewal we are hopefully expecting in these days of preparing for the third millennium.

ELEVEN

MARY: MODEL OF DISCIPLESHIP
The Resurrection Through Pentecost

"If anyone serves me, he must follow me."
JOHN 12:26

*"Mary is more blessed in her discipleship
than in her motherhood."*
St. Augustine

When our thoughts turn to Mary, her role of motherhood immediately comes to mind, and rightly so. She is the Mother of Jesus and she is the Mother of his Body, the Church. She is also our Mother. But in the economy of salvation Mary fulfills another important role: she is the first and perfect disciple of Jesus. Mary fulfilled every aspect of discipleship. In this calling she is also our model and exemplar.

What Makes a Disciple?

When Jesus began his teaching mission, he called people to follow him, to listen to his teaching, to learn more about him and the way of life he was proclaiming. Only after this orientation could they become disciples.

A disciple is more than a follower. A follower is somewhat like a student who learns by listening to the teaching of a professor, either lecture-style or under the tutelage and instruction of a teacher. A disciple, on the other hand, observes the lifestyle of the master and follows him so closely that eventually he will be identified with the master. The disciple too learns by listening, but also by living close to the master in order to learn by observation. The disciple carefully observes his master as he relates to other people, as he meets every situation in daily living. He strives to capture the mentality, the attitudes, the feelings, the heart of the master in order to become like him.

The followers of Jesus were called to be his disciples. At times even seemingly unlikely people were singled out as potential disciples. Jesus invited Matthew to "follow me," (Mt 9:9). Matthew got up and followed, and so the tax gatherer became one of the twelve apostles. Unworthy or not, we too are being invited to follow Jesus. This is our call: to listen to his teaching, to observe his actions and attitudes, to be imbued with his mind and heart.

Three Steps to Discipleship

The call. The call to discipleship comes from the Lord. As Jesus explained, "You did not choose me, but I chose you" (Jn 15:16).

The call of Jesus to Matthew is a universal call to all of us to become his disciples. In the Gospel of John, Jesus said: "If anyone serves me, he must follow me," (Jn 12:26). The Father clearly states the prime condition for authentic discipleship: "You shall be holy, for I the Lord your God am holy" (Lev 19:2). We are all called to live a committed Christian way of life, regardless of our station in life. The Lord calls each of us to a special ministry that will naturally lead us along different avenues on our journey to a deeper, more personal union with him.

It may happen that what sometimes appears to be a call from the Lord may require some prayer and guidance of the Holy Spirit to determine its authenticity. There is a possibility that what seems to be a call may lead us away from the Lord rather than to him. Our personal desires may silence the inner voice of the Lord. A father may feel an urge to participate in a worthwhile program that would leave him little time with his family. Likewise, a mother with children at home may feel drawn to volunteer her time and talent in good but time-consuming ways that require considerable time away from her children. Both of these apparent calls must be discerned more fully to determine if they are truly from God, or if the desire comes from our own desires.

A disciple is called to walk more closely with the Lord so that his or her mind and heart may be transformed and be identified with the mind and heart of Jesus. As disciples, we may be called to more intense prayer, or to listen to the Lord communicating with us in his Word, especially in the Gospels. The Lord may also be reminding us to be more patient, loving, or understanding, or to show more concern for others. While a call to discipleship is ongoing, the pathways may vary from time to time as the Lord calls us to different ministries.

A certain person may experience a call to a longer or a lifetime commitment, be it to live a single life, or to enter the married state, or feel some inclination to serve God and others in the religious life. To discern any of these major calls to discipleship, a person must spend time in quiet prayer, seeking the guidance of the Holy Spirit. It is also wise to seek the advice of a competent spiritual director or other mature spiritual person.

Mary, our Mother, was especially called by God to be an ideal disciple. She was called and prepared from all eternity. In the Liturgy of the Word in the "Mass of the Blessed Virgin Mary," the Church applies the words of St. Paul to Mary:

Those whom he predestined he also called; and those whom he called he also justified; and those whom he justified he also glorified. ROMANS 8:30

These words aptly apply to Mary and the unique role to which she was called. Mary was predestined by God to be immaculately conceived so that no stain of sin could mar the dwelling place of the Lord of heaven and earth. The Father justified Mary so that she could become the Mother of his Son. The fruits of the redemption were preapplied to her. The salvific mission of the Church began with this justification of Mary. This was Mary's glorification.

Mary's personal call into discipleship—the moment when she was faced with the choice of saying yes or no to the work God had been preparing her for—took place at the Annunciation. This was God's immediate, direct call to Mary—when the angel Gabriel appeared to her and asked her to become the Mother of the Messiah. There could have been no mistaking the privileged call of the Lord.

While it is true that the words of St. Paul to the Romans are frequently applied to Mary and her unique vocation as the Mother of the Messiah, these words are meant for all of us as well. We, too, are called by God to a special vocation. Just as God predestined, justified, and glorified Mary, he knew from all eternity that he would call us to be his disciples in a given apostolate. God has not only predestined us from all eternity, but, if we are receptive and cooperative with his grace, he will justify us and lead us into our glorification as well.

Conditioning and conversion. When God calls anyone to fulfill a precise role in his plans, a conditioning process and conversion are always necessary, since we are so hampered by our myopic humanness. This takes time, patience, endurance, and faithfulness.

For some people a conversion may mean turning away from a

life of sin and being reconciled to God. In the context of disciple-ship, however, conversion includes a more complete turning to God by keeping ourselves mindful of his abiding presence with us and within us. This awareness will better dispose us to recognize his will in all the happenings of life. It will also condition us by helping us to curb our judgmental attitudes, to refrain from idle or malicious gossip. This will enable us to reflect the gentleness and kindness of Jesus.

Accepting disappointments, misunderstandings, criticism, or rejection is a form of suffering. If it is accepted cheerfully, it will help us to mature spiritually and to become better disciples.

In our own lives we have discovered that when all is going well and no problems or anxieties beset us, and we enjoy good health, our awareness of God is more remote. On the other hand, suffer-ing of any kind will sober our thoughts and bring us closer to the Lord. God permits various kinds of suffering to help us to become more mature disciples ourselves, and thus to influence others by our peaceful, joyful Christian mentality.

Suffering will also remain a mystery, but history records the fact that many of the people that the Lord chose to be special disciples have been conditioned through suffering for their important min-istries. St. Ignatius of Loyola, St. Teresa of Avila, and St. Francis of Assisi are good examples of this.

As we saw in the last chapter, Mary was not exempt from the conditioning process, and neither was Joseph. In spite of the fact that God had chosen these two privileged people, they still required more preparation and conditioning. It came with much pain and anxiety—especially during the time of Mary's mysterious pregnancy. God permitted this testing of Mary and Joseph in order to strengthen their faith and trust, so that they would respond readily to whatever he might ask of them.

If we follow the footsteps of Mary from the moment of her Annunciation onward, we discover that her life was filled with dif-ficulties and trials. These she lovingly accepted as a part of her vocation. Mary walked the walk of faith. She persevered through all the difficulties and pain, which, being totally human, she experienced fully though she was sinless. Mary paid a high price to become and remain a faithful disciple.

Commitment. After we have been called and conditioned by the Lord, we arrive at the third stage of becoming a full-fledged disciple—our personal commitment to the Lord.

There are, of course, different levels of commitment. Our commitment may be a long-term resolve to accept and fulfill the will of God by keeping our minds and wills in tune with the Lord, come what may. When our saying "Yes" to the Lord is difficult, even to the point of tears, our commitment is not invalidated by our conflicting human emotions. Instead we must rely even more on God's grace to help us in our resolve. We also need this grace to help us with specific or temporary commitments, such as when we promise to spend a certain amount of time each day in quiet, wordless prayer, or when we resolve to go to Mass daily during Lent. We will be more faithful to all these commitments if we pause frequently to review our life and to ask God for his grace to strengthen us.

Mary's life exemplifies all the facets of unselfish commitment to God. At the time of the Annunciation Mary's commitment seemed to come rather readily: "Behold, I am the handmaid of the Lord; let it be to me according to your word" (Lk 1:38). This was not a sudden impulse on Mary's part. From her earliest years the Lord was preparing her to give her unconditional "fiat." Since no stain of sin marred her beautiful soul, Mary was the special temple of the Holy Spirit who was dynamic within her, transforming her so that she could fulfill the mission to which she was being called.

But Mary did her part to respond to God as the most committed of disciples. She was open and receptive to the Holy Spirit and must have spent hours in quiet prayer in her home in Nazareth.

Nazareth was a school of prayer. Here Mary contemplated the mysterious workings of God evolving in her life.

As Mary grew in the awareness of the love of the Father, Son, and Holy Spirit, she responded with an ever-increasing love as she submitted totally to the Lord's plans for her. She did so not out of a sense of duty or obligation, but as an expression of her love, which made her a perfect disciple.

Mary, True Disciple

What is it about Mary that makes her the perfect model of the dedicated disciple? Once when a woman in the crowd complimented Mary as the Mother of Jesus, Jesus pointed toward the answer. The woman cried out:

> "Blessed is the womb that bore you and the breasts that nursed you!" But he said, "Blessed rather are those who hear the word of God and obey it."   LUKE 11:27-28, NRSV

By these words Jesus revealed the real reason for Mary's blessedness: not the fact that Mary was chosen to be his Mother, but that she responded graciously and generously to her role by listening to God's Word and living in accord with that Word. This has been a long-standing interpretation among biblical scholars. In *The Jerome Biblical Commentary*, noted biblical scholar Fr. Carroll Stuhlmuller, C.P., summarizes this belief:

> Jesus now gives the true sign of holiness, "hear the word of God and keep it." Not even the greatest external honor (being Jesus' mother) sufficed. Mary is "blessed" for pondering God's word.[1]

St. Augustine leaves no doubt about why Mary is truly blessed:

Indeed, the blessed Mary certainly did the Father's will, and so it was for her a greater thing to have been Christ's disciple than to have been his Mother, and she is more blessed in her discipleship than in her motherhood.[2]

On another occasion when Jesus was teaching a large crowd who gathered to hear him, he was told that his mother and brothers wanted to see him but could not reach him because of the crowd. Jesus' response highlighted Mary's spiritual motherhood as more important than her natural maternity: "Whoever does the will of my Father in heaven is my brother, and sister, and mother" (Mt 12:46-50).

In *The Jerome Biblical Commentary*, Fr. John L. McKenzie, S.J., a recognized and respected biblical scholar, explains what Jesus meant:

The new unity Jesus forms about himself is a unity in which other bonds of kinship are sublimated. Jesus does not reject the bonds of kinship, but raises all who believe in him to an intimacy of kinship. His own kin exclude themselves from this new unity if they do not believe in him.[3]

Mary listened to the word of God and let it become the guiding norm of her life. This is what made her the perfect disciple.

The Cost of Discipleship

Jesus does not trick anyone into following him and becoming his disciple. "I am with you always," he promises (Mt 28:20), but he also cautions us plainly that the life of a disciple may be difficult at times: "If any man would come after me, let him deny himself and take up his cross daily and follow me" (Lk 9:23).

We must be detached from purely earthly attachments in order to be open and pliable to the will of God. The cross of which Jesus speaks is not always pain and suffering, but includes daily demands and duties performed with love and dedication.

Jesus gave us some clear insights into the requirements for becoming his disciple. When a certain man wanted to follow him, Jesus warned that he could not offer any worldly glory: "Foxes have holes, and birds of the air have nests," he told him, "but the Son of man has nowhere to lay his head." When another person asked if he could stay at home until his father died, Jesus replied, "Leave the dead to bury their own dead; but as for you, go and proclaim the kingdom of God." To another would-be disciple Jesus said: "No one who puts a hand to the plough and looks back is fit for the kingdom of God" (Lk 9:57-62).

St. Mark records one such incident, in which Jesus encounters a rich young man who wanted to be his disciple.

Jesus, looking at him, loved him and said, "You lack one thing; go, sell what you have, and give to the poor, and you will have treasure in heaven; and come and follow me."   MARK 10:21

Elsewhere Jesus gives a stark image of what it costs to be his disciple: "Truly, truly, I say to you, unless a grain of wheat falls into the earth and dies, it remains alone; but if it dies, it bears much fruit" (Jn 12:24).

To Serve As Jesus Served

As we listen to the words of Jesus we may get the impression that the requirements for discipleship are too stringent and unreasonable. Why did Jesus seem to emphasize only the hardships and privations his disciple would have to endure? Why did he lay down such uninviting conditions?

One reason, perhaps, is that Jesus wanted to make it very clear that what *he* meant by discipleship might be very different from his followers' preconceived notions. Jesus' disciples were not to expect honors in this life—no high places at table, no public acclaim of their piety, no respect for their giving all to follow Jesus. They were not even to set their hearts on having the most important places in the kingdom of God!

It was important for Jesus to clarify his conditions for discipleship because at that time there were various false notions about the Messiah. Some people hoped and believed that the Messiah would free them from the domination of Rome. They expected him to make them a powerful nation once again, as in the days of King David. As the long-awaited Messiah, Jesus wanted it to be known that such worldly ambitions had no place in his spiritual kingdom.

Rather, the essence of discipleship in the kingdom that Jesus announced is service. Not only are Jesus' followers not to lord it over other people: they are to put themselves at the service of others, especially the most humble. In Jesus' kingdom, even leadership—especially leadership—means service. Jesus set the pace when he washed the feet of the apostles in the Upper Room before the Last Supper. On that occasion he said:

> Do you know what I have done to you? You call me Teacher and Lord; and you are right, for so I am. If I, then, your Lord and Teacher, have washed your feet, you also ought to wash one another's feet. For I have given you an example, that you also should do as I have done to you. JOHN 13:12-15

Disciples of the Risen Christ

Following Jesus in his example of service would be hopelessly impossible were it not for the Resurrection. But because the

Resurrection gives us a share in the very life of God, it enables us not just to follow Jesus but to become like him. As we travel the road of discipleship, there will be formed within us the mind and heart of the One who invites us to "learn from me, for I am gentle and lowly in heart" (Mt 11:29).

If we are to become full-fledged disciples of Jesus, and learn from him who is gentle and humble of heart, we must recognize who we are and to what we are called to be. As disciples we are empowered to fulfill our mission in life only because the Lord is living in us, inspiring, enlightening, encouraging, and strengthening us. These are some of the fruits of his Resurrection and of our rising with him.

Throughout his writing and preaching, St. Paul echoes the joy and jubilation of his heart when he speaks about the Resurrection of Jesus and of our rising.

> Do you not know that all of us who have been baptized into Christ Jesus were baptized into his death? We were buried therefore with him by baptism into his death, so that as Christ was raised from the dead by the glory of the Father, we too might walk in newness of life. ROMANS 6:3-4

The "newness of life" is the exalted, risen life that Jesus shares with us. Because we are human we are hampered from understanding and receiving this fully. We will share more fully in the divine life and love of Christ when the Lord calls us to our eternal reward.

St. Paul reminds us that when sin entered our world, the human race severed its relationship with God. But through the redemptive death and resurrection of Jesus, our personal relationship with our loving Father was restored. St. Paul puts it this way:

> The death he died, he died to sin, once for all, but the life he lives he lives to God. So you also must consider yourselves dead to sin and alive to God in Christ Jesus. ROMANS 6:10

Again, in writing to the Galatians, Paul extols one of the blessed fruits of the resurrection in his own life: "It is no longer I who live, but Christ who lives in me; and the life I now live in the flesh I live by faith in the Son of God, who loved me and gave himself for me" (Gal 2:20).

As we become more aware of the boundless love of God and his infinite goodness to us, it will make us humble and docile and keep us more alert to our total dependence upon him. In order to respond to the outpouring of the Lord's blessings upon us, he asks only for the gift of ourselves to him in all we think, do, and say. St. Paul asks us to make this oblation of self when he urges us to "yield yourselves to God as men who have been brought from death to life, and your members to God as instruments of righteousness" (Rom 6:13-14).

As we reflect on the unfathomable goodness of the Lord in raising us to new life and preparing us for its fullness at the time of our deaths, our constant prayer should be that of St. Paul:

I want to know Christ and the power of his resurrection and the sharing of his sufferings by becoming like him in death, if somehow I may attain the resurrection from the dead.

PHILIPPIANS 3:10-11, NRSV

The teachings of Scripture about the resurrection of Jesus and its marvelous fruits that have come down to us throughout the ages are set forth in summary in *The Catechism of the Catholic Church:*

The Paschal mystery has two aspects: by his death, Christ liberates us from sin; by his Resurrection, he opens for us the way to a new life. This new life is above all justification that reinstates us in God's grace, "so that as Christ was raised from the dead by the glory of the Father, we too might walk in newness of life." Justification consists in both victory over the death caused by sin and a new participation in grace. It brings about filial adoption so that men become Christ's brethren, as Jesus himself called his disciples after his Resurrection....[4]

On our journey in life, these truths bring us great hope, peace, and joy. Little wonder that St. Paul's heart resonated with so much joy and jubilation!

Mary and the Resurrection

If we are concerned that there is no mention of Mary in the fifty post-Resurrection days, we need to recall that Scripture is written not primarily as an historical account, but as a record of the truths and way of life we are to follow.

Scripture does not relate any appearance of Jesus to his Mother on the day of the Resurrection. However, many saints and mystics throughout Church history have assumed that it did in fact happen. In the "Spiritual Exercises of St. Ignatius" he, who is meticulous in supporting his teachings with Scripture, says in the contemplation on the Resurrection of Jesus:

He appeared to the Virgin Mary. Though this is not mentioned explicitly in Scripture, it must be considered as stated when Scripture says that "he appeared to many others." Knowing the mutual love that flowed from the heart of Jesus and Mary, is there any doubt about such an appearance?[5]

We do not find any mention of Mary in Scripture after the Resurrection until we meet her in the Upper Room, awaiting the coming of the Holy Spirit (see Acts 1:14). Because of her strong, dynamic, operative faith, Mary certainly played an important role during this fifty-day interim. Her own faith and trust no doubt was a great influence on many others.

As Mary brought comfort and hope to so many after the Resurrection, she was fulfilling her role as a disciple of Jesus. Mary's role also fulfilled one of the primary objectives of the millennial renewal: giving witness to the presence and power of the Lord dwelling within her. Her sinlessness gave her a deeper appreciation of the tremendous blessings that flowed from the triumphant Resurrection of Jesus.

Having experienced a deep love relationship with the Lord, Mary was ecstatic with joy and delight, realizing that the whole human race was redeemed, and that those who believed and followed him would share in the divine life and love of the Lord. As we follow the Lord and enter into that same deep love relationship, we, too, can experience the joy that Mary experienced when Jesus rose from the dead.

The faith and trust, the hope and gratitude that overflowed from Mary's heart radiated to everyone she met during those jubilant days. This was her personal mission, which she—as our spiritual Mother—continues in this time of Great Renewal. She is the "Star" who safely guides our steps to the Lord. As our Mother, Mary is deeply concerned about our spiritual welfare and our eternal destiny. For this reason we frequently pray: "Pray for us sinners now and at the hour of our death."

Service Builds on Love

Jesus made it very clear that love has to be the motivating factor in making both an initial and an ongoing decision to follow in his footsteps. Love must be the foundation of our commitment to a life of service to the Lord and to others. If love is not the focus, the impelling reason and the power motivating our discipleship, we will soon abandon our Master out of fear, discouragement, weariness, or some other temptation.

But what kind of love must characterize a disciple of Jesus? The answer is summed up in the two great commandments: we must love God with all our heart, soul, mind, and strength; and love our neighbor as ourselves (see Mk 12:30-31). Speaking to the apostles at the Last Supper, Jesus gave this second commandment a personal twist for anyone who would follow him as a disciple: "Love one another as I have loved you." And lest we miss the point of what that love entails, Jesus went on to specify: "Greater love has no man than this: that a man lay down his life for his friends" (Jn 15:13).

Love for God comes through knowing him, and knowing him means encountering his love, which awakens our own. In fact, only when we know the Lord as a loving, caring, personal God can we love him. "We love, because he first loved us" (1 Jn 4:19).

The most effective way to know God with our heart is to listen in wordless prayer to what he is saying to us. Meditating on Scripture—pondering the episodes of Jesus' life on earth—also stirs our love. St. Teresa of Avila says we must know the human Jesus in order to love him. We come to know him as we accompany him in spirit through the Gospels—listening to his words, observing his actions, trying to understand his sentiments as he meets people and carries out his ministry.

The Power of Pentecost

To love others as Jesus has loved us—what a challenge! And again, one that would have been impossible if Jesus had not come to our aid. "I will pray the Father," Jesus promised, and he will send the Holy Spirit, who "will teach you all things, and bring to your remembrance all that I have said to you" (Jn 14:16, 26).

In particular, the coming of the Holy Spirit means that we become capable of the kind of love Jesus calls us to: "God's love has been poured into our hearts through the Holy Spirit who has been given to us" (Rom 5:5).

The Upper Room is where the Spirit's transforming power was first made manifest, and among the disciples gathered there was one who knew full well how much this divine power could do! Mary had experienced the Holy Spirit's work throughout her whole lifetime. Molded and transformed by the Spirit, Mary knew how much the apostles and other disciples would benefit from the Spirit's coming.

How fervently Mary prayed for ten days in that Upper Room! How earnestly she asked the Holy Spirit to come upon her fellow disciples to gift and endow them with the enlightenment and power they would need for the ministry and commission which her son had given them. We can well assume that Mary's firm faith and fervent prayer for the Spirit's outpouring were an inspiration to all those who had assembled and were anxiously awaiting the fulfillment of Jesus' promise.

Love Finds a Way

The love that the Holy Spirit poured out into the hearts of the waiting disciples—the love he readily pours out into our own—is an unselfish love that makes discipleship a joy.

When we love someone unselfishly, we long to be in the presence of that person, to visit and to share with him or her. We are always eager to do everything to please the one we love. In fact, we even try to anticipate their wishes and needs. Love gives us a deep insight into the personality and dispositions of the person we love. Intuitively we recognize what the person needs or desires without a word being spoken.

No task or burden is too great for such love to undertake. At the tomb of Jesus on the day of the Resurrection, Mary Magdalene made a rather rash statement to the person she thought was the gardener. Thinking that he had removed Jesus' body from the tomb, she said to him, "Tell me where you have laid him, and I will take him away" (Jn 20:15). It did not occur to Mary Magdalene that she would probably not be able to lift such a heavy weight! Love knows no bounds.

Love in Action Today

A friend of mine was on a business trip to the Philippines. While there he wanted to visit a Maryknoll sister, whom we both knew. When he found her caring for a person in an advanced stage of leprosy, he said to her: "Sister, I would not do that for a million dollars."

With a twinkle in her eye she responded, "Neither would I." Motivated by genuine love, Sister was a true disciple.

A Maryknoll priest in Bolivia had an expansive mission territory. A huge mountain slide had obliterated a whole village, leaving only one survivor, a little boy who was badly hurt. The priest took him to his home and gently cared for him. One day the boy said to him, "Father, Jesus must have been like you." With Mary as his exemplar this priest also loved a great deal, which had enabled him to become a dedicated disciple of Jesus.

We are all called to be disciples by giving witness to our dedication to the Lord. There are many ways to do this: a husband who loves and respects his wife is demonstrating an invaluable lesson to his children. Business and professional people whose principles reflect honesty, integrity, and genuine concern for others witness powerfully for the Christian way of life. The uncomplaining mother who smiles easily and retains a good sense of humor touches both her own family and everyone she encounters. Teachers who reveal a personal concern for their pupils are also real disciples of the Lord. In these ways and many others, we are to bring the love of Christ to our world.

Calling All Disciples!

The Lord has invited every one of us to become not only his follower but a dedicated disciple. As we have seen, the secret to discipleship—the eagerness to give ourselves totally, the willingness to deny ourselves, to take up our cross daily, to ourselves like the grain of wheat—is to love with an unconditional, enduring love. Such love is also what will enable us to carry out Jesus' call to minister to others: "I give you a new commandment, that you love one another. Just as I have loved you, you should love one another. By this everyone will know that you are my disciples, if you have love for one another," (Jn 13: 34-35, NRSV).

As we prepare to be more faithful disciples of Jesus for the new millennium, let us take Mary as our model of the love we seek. Mary's love was so intense that she could not refrain from giving herself generously and graciously to whatever the Lord willed for her. Mary committed herself without any hesitation or reservation, nor did she ever renege or even waver from her original promise. With Mary, it was always yes, whatever the call, whatever the difficulties.

Like Mary, our mission in life is to say yes to the Lord in all the happenings of every day. With her help, may our own daily yes to God express our willingness to accept and fulfill his will and to serve all those he sends our way.

Above all, let us be motivated by love. By intensifying our love for God, we will deepen our love for ourselves and love for our neighbor. In the apostolic letter, we are urged to bring ourselves to "a renewed appreciation of the presence and activity of the [Holy] Spirit" who is the very source of love.[6] Later on, Pope John Paul II observes: "The whole of the Christian life is like a great pilgrimage to the house of the Father, whose unconditional love for every human creature... we discover anew each day."[7]

The primary objectives of the Great Renewal will not be accomplished without the motivating power of love. That love is available to all of us if we are willing to reach out and grasp it.

TWELVE

MARY: QUEEN OF PEACE
The Assumption and Intercession of Mary

"Great peace have those who love thy law."
PSALMS 119:165

"To Jesus through Mary."
ST. LOUIS DE MONTFORT

O n Mount Zion, near Jerusalem, stands an imposing shrine called the Church of Dormition, which is staffed by the Benedictine monks. This shrine was built to commemorate the place where, according to tradition, Mary fell asleep at the end of her earthly life. According to the same tradition, Our Lady was carried from here to a crypt in the Valley of Kidron and laid to rest. From here she was taken body and soul into heaven.

Though Mary's assumption is not mentioned in Scripture, Christians since the time of the apostles have believed this truth. The Church presents this teaching in *The Catechism of the Catholic Church:*

The Most Blessed Virgin Mary, when the course of her earthly life was completed, was taken up body and soul into the glory of heaven, where she already shares in the glory of her Son's

Resurrection, anticipating the resurrection of all members of his Body.[1]

Proclaiming this truth officially in 1950, Pope Pius XII reminded us:

In their homilies and sermons on this feast, the holy fathers and great doctors spoke of the assumption of the Mother of God as something familiar and accepted by the faithful.... Above all, they brought out more clearly the fact that what is commemorated on this feast is not simply the total absence of corruption from the dead body of Blessed Virgin Mary, but also her triumph over death and her glorification in heaven, after the pattern set by her Son, Jesus Christ.[2]

We make a distinction between Jesus' entry into glory and Mary's going to heaven. We call Jesus' leaving this world his Ascension into heaven, since he was raised by his own power, whereas Mary was taken into heaven, not by her own power but by the power of God. This is why we call Mary's leaving this world her *assumption* rather than *ascension* into heaven.

Each year on August 15 when we celebrate Mary's assumption into heaven, we are reminded of our own eternal destiny as planned by the infinite love of God. It instills within us an expectant faith and a vibrant hope as we look forward to the incredible fruits of the Resurrection awaiting us.

"Remember, O Most Gracious Virgin Mary..."

Through her Assumption Mary entered body and soul into heaven, where her Son sits in glory at the right hand of the Father. Sometimes as we consider Jesus in his glory—resting in the perfect love of the Trinity, receiving the praise of all the heavenly hosts as well as the honor, praise, and glory rising from his earth-bound people—we might imagine Our Lord as rather far removed from us. Nothing could be further from the truth. The glory of Jesus consists in continuing his redemptive ministry of healing, forgiving, caring, providing, and loving us until the end of time.

In the same way, Mary's mission among us on earth did not terminate with her glorious Assumption into heaven. The Second Vatican Council explained that Mary's role as our mother will last without interruption until we too have entered into heavenly glory: "Taken up to heaven, she did not lay aside this saving office but by her manifold intercession continues to bring us the gifts of eternal salvation."[3]

Mary's many appearances on earth are one sign of her ongoing love and concern for all her pilgrim people. And in our own personal lives, who of us has not experienced Mary's powerful intercession at the throne of God? Like millions before us we readily turn to Mary with confidence, in familiar prayers like the Memorare and the Hail Mary.

Mary Presents Jesus

Mary's intercessory role, as the Second Vatican Council clearly explained, "in no way obscures or diminishes the unique mediation of Christ, but rather shows its power."[4] Mary's influence flows from and depends completely on the merits of her Son.

Mary never seeks to eclipse Jesus; she always points us in his direction and works to bring us to him. "When she is being preached and venerated, she summons the faithful to her Son and his sacrifice, and to love for the Father."[5]

During her sojourn on earth and throughout the centuries since her assumption into heaven, Mary has faithfully and consistently fulfilled her special mission of presenting Jesus to anyone who is seeking a deeper, more personal relationship with the Lord. Now, in this age of the Great Renewal of the third millennium, Mary is eager to lead all people into an intimate heart-knowledge of her son which will enable them to love him and to live in conformity with his divine will.

One of the principal roles of Mary in this time of the third millennium is to present Jesus, the Prince of Peace. Before we examine God's gift of peace, which is such an important part of Mary's intercession for us, let us review a few of the gospel passages in which Mary is called upon to present her son to those who seek him. Mary's faithfulness throughout these vignettes should strengthen our confidence in our Mother's loving desire to present Jesus to us as well.

Into the Hill Country

Mary is a real "Christopher" (Christ-bearer) bringing her unborn son into the home of Zechariah and Elizabeth (see Lk 1:39-56). John the Baptist, as yet unborn, acknowledges the divine presence by stirring in his mother's womb. John's reaction strengthens the faith of Elizabeth:

> And Elizabeth was filled with the Holy Spirit and she exclaimed with a loud cry: "Blessed are you among women, and blessed is the fruit of your womb. And why is this granted to me, that the mother of my Lord should come to me?"   LUKE 1:41-43

Just as Jesus was present in the house of Zechariah, he is present with us and within us—invisible, but no less real. We must keep ourselves aware that this is not an imagined presence but a faith presence.

In many of her appearances throughout the years, Mary reminds us of the Lord's abiding presence and urges us to live daily in his presence. As Jesus reached out through Mary to

Elizabeth and John, so he continues to do so through Mary, especially through her numerous appearances and messages.

City of David

Each time we contemplate the scene at Bethlehem, our hearts are moved with sentiments of gratitude, wonder, joy, and love. When Mary presented her Child in this impoverished setting, it was to different types of people who had varying levels of faith.

Joseph (see Mt 1:18-25). When the angel visited Joseph some months before the birth of Jesus, Joseph's faith was increased. He was enabled to understand in a limited way the tremendous mystery which was taking place in his and Mary's life.

When Mary presented her son to him, Joseph was filled with reverence, awed at the unfathomable depths of God's love for his people. Joseph was the first to adore his incarnate God, and as he did, his own heart overflowed with a loving response.

The shepherds (see Lk 2:8-20). The shepherds, like all Israelites, had a deep longing for the coming of the promised Messiah. Even though their work in the fields with their flocks day and night prevented them from worshiping regularly in the temple and also hindered them from studying the Scriptures and prophecies concerning the coming of the Messiah, they believed and trusted that God would fulfill their longing.

The shepherds' faith was sufficiently vibrant that they believed the message of the angel and decided, "Let us go over to Bethlehem and see this thing that has happened, which the Lord has made known to us" (Lk 2:15). Their faith, which urged them to come, was rewarded as they saw the Child and began to understand.

The shepherds found great peace and joy, and they "returned, glorifying and praising God for all they had heard and seen" (Lk

2:20). When Mary presented Jesus to them, their faith was greatly enkindled and their longing and expectations were fulfilled.

Magi from the East (see Mt 2:1-12). There were stirrings of faith in the hearts of the Magi, but they were still searching as they studied the stars and all that the heavens proclaimed. At great personal sacrifice, they made the arduous journey to Bethlehem. They came to pay their respects to "he who has been born king of the Jews." As they explained: "We have seen his star in the East, and have come to worship him" (Lk 2:2).

The Magi had some understanding of the identity and mission of the newborn king, for they brought him gifts: gold, to acknowledge his kingship; frankincense, the gift for a priest; and myrrh, the gift for one who is to die. After their visit with Herod and the warning they received in a dream, "they departed to their own country by another way" (Lk 2:12).

We can be certain that the Magi not only traveled away from Bethlehem by another route but also that they followed another path throughout their whole lives after Mary presented the Child Jesus to them. Surely the Lord filled the Magi with greater faith, joy, high hopes, and expectations, along with the peace which only he can give.

Enemies (see Mt 2:16-18). There were also those who came to Bethlehem without any faith and with brutal intentions. Mary did not present her Child to these people, of course, but shielded and protected him from them.

Cruel soldiers arrived in Bethlehem to massacre all boys in the vicinity who were two years old and under. They had been sent by Herod, who was furious that his insidious scheme had been thwarted by the Magi. In his jealous rage and fear of losing his throne, Herod did not realize that God's plans cannot be thwarted. Jesus escaped, and the horrible massacre of the infants made them the first martyrs and saints of the Christian era.

Yesterday, today, and forever. People of all types, with various levels of faith, still travel in spirit to the humble abode in Bethlehem. Do we find ourselves among them?

In spirit let us visit with *Joseph.* He stood silently, wrapped in wonder at the divine mystery taking place before his eyes. As Mary presented her newborn Babe, Joseph must certainly have had a genuine mystical experience. As we, too, contemplate the unfolding of God's plan in the mystery of the Incarnation, we readily recall the words of the Gospel: "For God so loved the world that he gave his only Son, that whoever believes in him should not perish but have eternal life" (Jn 3:16). In silence and solitude we bask in the sunshine of God's love; in wordless prayer our love flows out to God.

On occasions when our faith and trust in the Lord are challenged and we hesitate to respond to his will, we can go in spirit to visit Bethlehem in the company of the *shepherds.* Because of their trusting, obedient response to the angels' message, their faith was greatly increased. As we listen to the shepherds praising and glorifying God on their way back to their flocks, our own spirit will be lifted with joyous praise and gratitude to God for his incomprehensible goodness to us in sending us his Son and calling Mary to present him to us.

When we experience an emptiness, a lack of fulfillment, or grave frustrations in our lives, the example of the *Magi* may speak to us most powerfully. We may feel all alone and yearn for a deeper awareness of the Lord. He may seem far afield when pain, hardships, and difficulties arise. Distractions, preoccupation, busyness, or sheer neglect may erase any awareness of the abiding presence and love of the Lord.

When such sentiments plague us, we can in spirit observe the Magi as they make the arduous journey to Bethlehem and pay homage to Jesus. As we do, we will be reminded that the Lord asks only one gift of us. It is the gift of ourselves—made with trust, humility, and dependence upon him, and especially the gift of keeping our will always in tune with his mind and heart.

As Mary accepted the gifts of the Magi in the name of her son, she also accepts the gift of ourselves to our Lord and Savior. Do we not pray daily: "O Jesus, through the Immaculate Heart of Mary, I offer all my prayers, works, joys, and sufferings of this day..."? When we graciously and generously offer our gift of self to the Lord, we will find that, like the Magi, we too are traveling "another road"—one that is filled with love, peace, and joy.

As for the *enemies of Christ*, they continue to live in our society today. They reject the Lord and strive by devious means to lead others away from him. Yet how much our heavenly Mother longs to present Jesus to these people too! We join our prayers for them with Mary's, imploring the Holy Spirit to touch their hardened hearts and lead them to a complete conversion during the days of the Great Renewal.

Given the brokenness of our human nature, we can all too easily turn a deaf ear to the promptings of the Holy Spirit in the course of each day. Our pride and self-sufficiency often weaken our resolve to unite ourselves more closely with the Person of Jesus. Our wayward tendencies may influence us to such an extent that we fall into sin. We have no intention of alienating ourselves from God, but in a moment of weakness we may succumb. Inadvertently our words, actions, and attitudes may have a pejorative effect on others, impeding or even interrupting their "great pilgrimage to the house of the Father." To alert ourselves to these possible happenings in our lives, spiritual writers urge us to daily review our lives, to consider whether there is a need for caution or concern in some area.

Presentation in the Temple

Mary's most formal presentation of Jesus took place when she and Joseph "brought him to Jerusalem to present him to the Lord, as it is written in the law of the Lord" (Lk 2:22-38). This fulfillment of the requirements of the Law manifested publicly Jesus' total dedication to fulfill the will of the Father throughout his sojourn on earth.

After this ceremony Mary made personal presentations of the Child Jesus to two devout people who were praying in the temple. Simeon, a just and pious man, had been promised by the Holy Spirit that he would see the Messiah before he died. How overjoyed and consoled Simeon was to see Jesus! His beautiful prayer of resignation—"Lord, now lettest thou thy servant depart in peace..." (Lk 2:29)—is prayed daily in the Night Prayer of the Liturgy of the Hours.

Mary then presented Jesus to Anna, a prophetess who "did not depart from the temple, worshiping with fasting and prayer night and day" (Lk 2:37). Anna became a special messenger of the Lord, for she "gave thanks to God and spoke of him to all who were looking for the redemption of Jerusalem" (Lk 2:38). Her joy brought much hope, comfort, and consolation to a waiting world.

Both Anna and Simeon encourage us, each in their own way, to seek the Lord persistently. Simeon's example of prayerful waiting for the Lord speaks of the importance of the wordless, listening prayer of the heart. Anna inspires us to await the Lord with prayer and fasting and motivates us to make Jesus known by our words, actions, and attitudes. Contemplating this pair as they recognize Jesus in his Mother's arms can also make us deeply grateful for the precious gift of faith which has been given us.

In the Shadow of the Cross

Other episodes from Jesus' life—his "lost and found" experience in the temple, his departure from Nazareth, his first miracle at Cana—also can be viewed as Mary's presentation of her son. The scene on Calvary's hill, however, is the most dramatic presentation of them all (see Jn 19:25-30). In fact, this solemn episode includes two presentations, one explicit and one implied.

Jesus presents Mary. Jesus was aware that we would need a model to help us struggle on toward heaven. He also knew that we would need the love, care, and concern of a spiritual Mother who would be ever solicitous about all our needs. This is why, from the cross, Jesus presented us with a treasure far beyond anything we could have expected: "Behold, your Mother" (Jn 19:27).

These words have deep symbolic meaning, for the "beloved disciple" to whom they are spoken represents everyone throughout the ages who follows Jesus faithfully. From that moment on Calvary and for all time, Mary, calling on the words of Scripture, tells us: "You are precious in my eyes, and honored, and I love you" (Is 43:4).

This may be considered a two-fold presentation. Jesus gave us his Mother as our model, exemplar, and companion on our pilgrimage throughout our earthly sojourn. He also provided for his Mother's protection: "Behold, your son" (Jn 19:26). This presentation was essential to provide for Mary's material needs as well as her protection: since Jesus died as a criminal, his enemies might have begun to persecute his mother as well. In this passage, Jesus was calling not only for John but for all his disciples to be a source of comfort and security for Mary.

Mary presents Jesus. Mary presents Jesus to us by reminding us of the infinite love he has for us, which prompted him to lay down his life for us: "Greater love has no man than this, that a man lay down his life for his friends" (Jn 15:13).

During those dreadful three hours when Jesus was on the cross, we see Mary "standing" near him. Her posture manifests her total union with Jesus. Mary's example is a source of inspiration and motivation, reminding us that we too can unite ourselves with Jesus in offering ourselves to the Father.

"Do this in remembrance of me," Jesus had said earlier, as he blessed and offered the bread and wine which would become his body and blood (see Lk 22:19-20). In this command to celebrate the Lord's Supper, we can also see Jesus' invitation to participate in his sacrifice on the cross. At Calvary Mary shows us how to do this graciously and generously, in complete union with Jesus' redemptive sacrifice. Mary's posture leads us to Jesus.

The Gift of Peace

Presenting Jesus, which is at the heart of Mary's motherly intercession, puts us in touch with the Giver of a gift for which every human heart longs: the peace which comes only from Jesus. As we come to know the Lord personally and live more in union with him, we will know a deep peace which will flow freely through us to many others.

But what exactly is peace? Certainly, people define it in a variety of ways. For some, peace means a cessation of all military hostilities, a time when no war is being waged. Others think of peace as a time of serenity and quiet, a time free from the usual strains and stresses, worries and anxieties which invariably beset the pathway of life. For a mother of young children, peace may mean that time when all the little ones are safely tucked in their beds and quiet reigns throughout the house. (I once saw a cartoon of a rather disheveled mother with her little daughter tugging at her skirt and asking: "Mother, why did you say that you would go crazy if I asked one more question?")

God of Peace

In the Old Testament our loving Father is known as the God of Peace. Gideon erected an altar to Yahweh-Shalom, God of Peace (see Jgs 6:24). God is implored and praised for his gift of peace in at least eighteen psalms. Hundreds of times he is called upon to grant his peace to his people.

Centuries before Jesus was incarnated into our world, the great prophet Isaiah foretold that the Messiah would come as the "Prince of Peace" (Is 9:6). When Jesus was born in Bethlehem, the angels announced his birth to the shepherds by designating his coming as a reign of peace. In the angelic chorus of praise they sang, "Glory to God in the highest, and on earth peace among men with whom he is pleased" (Lk 2:14). By his redemptive death and resurrection, Jesus reconciled the human family with God and bestowed his gift of peace upon it. As his farewell gift he bequeathed his peace to us: "Peace I leave with you; my peace I give to you; not as the world gives do I give to you" (Jn 14:27).

Jesus used the word "shalom," which means much more than our word "peace," as it is commonly translated. Shalom is a greeting and a blessing. It is a prayerful wish for all God's blessings culminating in his final blessing, eternal salvation.

Peace is one of the special fruits of the Holy Spirit which keeps our minds and hearts untroubled in the face of spiritual or temporal trials. It is a quiet euphoria, a tranquillity of mind and heart.

As mentioned in the first part of this book, peace is the fruit of good relationships on four different levels: peace with God, peace with ourselves, peace with our neighbor, and peace with all of creation. When we enjoy good relationships in all four areas, we will experience that genuine peace which the Lord wants us to have and which will eventually lead us to the incomprehensible peace of heaven. The Prince of Peace invites us to walk his way of life.

Mary Shows the Way

And who better than Mary, the Queen of Peace, to be our model and guide in each of the four areas where we must develop peaceful relationships?

From her tenderest years, Mary was imbued with the gift of peace by the Holy Spirit. The Preface of a special Mass, approved in 1987, that honors Mary as the Queen of Peace states: "She is the lowly handmaid, receiving your word from the angel Gabriel and conceiving in her virginal womb the Prince of Peace, Jesus Christ, your Son, our Lord." The Prince of Peace conceived by Mary restored peace to the human race by reconciling earth with heaven.

In writing to the Galatians and to us, St. Paul explains this restoration of peace: "But when the time had fully come, God sent forth his Son, born of woman, born under the law, to redeem those who were under the law, so that we might receive adoption as sons" (Gal 4:4).

In addition to the Incarnation, Mary also shared in the mystery of the Passion, which restored our severed relationship with the Father. Her heart was united with her son as he shed his blood to bring peace to a fallen people. Mary stood near the cross of Jesus and made the total oblation of herself, uniting it with the oblation of her son.

The Preface of the same Mass honoring Mary, Queen of Peace, reminds us of her sharing in Jesus' redemptive mission: "She is the faithful Mother, standing fearless beside the cross as her Son shed his blood for our salvation and reconciled all things to himself in peace." Mary's constant prayer is that we, her spiritual children, may know that peace which her son gained for us by his redemptive death on the cross.

By her example and intercession our Mother wants to lead us along the roadway to genuine peace, even at times when that peace seems hopelessly elusive. (Here it is worth recalling that it was in 1917, while the horrors of World War I raged throughout Europe, that Pope Benedict XV directed that the invocation "Queen of Peace" be added to the Litany of Loreto.) As we strive to imitate Mary in all our relationships, we will come to enjoy the fullness of peace.

Peace with God

The first and most important area in which we are to seek peace is in our relationship with God. Mary, our Queen of Peace, was always and totally at peace with God. The Holy Spirit had molded and transformed her sinless soul so that her will was always perfectly in tune with whatever God asked of her.

From her unhesitating yes to the Angel Gabriel to her union with her son's heart-rending sacrifice, Mary's whole attitude was always, "Let it be to me according to your word" (Lk 1:38). The psalmist's words, usually applied to Jesus, can also be applied to Mary: "I delight to do thy will, O my God; thy law is within my heart" (Ps 40:8). With this acquiescence to the Father's will, this total giving of herself to God's plan, Mary enjoyed perfect peace.

Our Way to Peace with God

The first step in trying to fulfill the will of God in our lives is to strive to the best of our ability to avoid sin of any kind. Unfortunately, our broken human nature is so prone to sin that we seem to fall often. In fact, our life seems to be a series of going from one conversion to another!

However, there is no room for discouragement (which is often the favorite tool of the Evil One). When we sin, our compassionate Father, like the father of the prodigal son, is waiting with open arms to receive us (see Lk 15:20). He reminds us: "I, I am He who blots out your transgressions for my own sake, and I will not remember your sins" (Is 43:25).

Jesus makes his forgiveness more personal when we meet him in the sacrament of reconciliation to receive his forgiving, healing love. When we encounter Jesus in this sacrament, which is often called the sacrament of pardon and peace, we are acknowledging him as our Savior and Redeemer and also recognizing our dire need of him. Jesus is happy to forgive us when we come to him humbly and sincerely, admitting our sins and asking his forgiveness. We can be certain that his pardon and peace will be ours in abundance.

In his bountiful goodness, God does even more for us. When we sin, the Lord teaches us humility and helps us to recognize our need for his help and grace. Thanks to his inexhaustible forbearance, he shows us how much we must depend on his divine help and become less reliant on ourselves. Strange as it may seem, sorrow and repentance for our sinfulness can be an occasion for growth in our spiritual life, so astounding is God's love for us.

When our sin is forgiven, the Holy Spirit can more easily mold and transform us, making us more receptive to accepting whatever the Lord may ask of us. We may have experienced certain times when we enjoyed the good feeling of knowing that we discerned and followed the promptings of the Holy Spirit. We may have found some delight in responding to the will of God, realizing that he is counting on us to assist him in implementing his plan in our times. The euphoria we enjoy springs from the peace of knowing that we are in tune with his divine will.

At times when difficulties, misunderstandings, or suffering of any kind arise, we may not be able to understand the Lord's plan and may even cry out, "Why, Lord? Why me, Lord? Why at this time, Lord?" In these circumstances, when our yes to the Lord is accompanied by an abundance of tears, we can call upon the Queen of Peace to intercede for us, that we may be able to give our consent as willingly and graciously as she did. And eventually we will discover that peace does exist even in pain.

Just as Mary's consent to the Lord played an important role in our salvation, our own acceptance—even if painful and reluctantly given—will bear much fruit for us and for many others without our being aware of it. When we reach this point, we have attained the first level of peace—peace with God, our Father.

Peace with Ourselves

In this area too, Mary is the best of models and guides. From her earliest years, our Blessed Mother was completely at peace with herself. She excelled so totally in accepting herself and her special mission that she will ever be an example and a challenge for us.

Mary was at peace and happy with the role to which the Lord called her. Her deep humility kept her attuned to God's will, and her profound love and desire to please him always kept her single-minded in doing whatever the Lord asked.

Mary gladly accepted her station in life, even though she was a poor, unlettered young woman from the country. In Galilee she lived a hidden life away from the various demands of society. Her life was confined for the most part to her little home in Nazareth, with only one excursion each year to Jerusalem to celebrate the Passover in the temple.

Mary gave no indication of self-pity when she was misunderstood and suspected by Joseph, nor when she suffered the loss of Jesus in the temple, nor even when she was plunged into her dreadful suffering on Calvary. Mary never protested against her lot in life, no matter how dull or difficult it was.

The Secret to Peace with Ourselves

God created us with a desire to be loved and appreciated by others. However, we are conscious of all our unlovable traits—our pride, selfishness, ambition, our judgmental attitude and our many unkindnesses to others, and a whole host of other shortcomings. We fear rejection while our heart cries out for acceptance and recognition.

In our insecurity we often strive to be someone we are not. We are convinced that if we were more talented and gifted, more popular and wealthy, we would be accepted and loved by everyone. Lacking these desired traits, we may become frustrated, disappointed, defensive. In a word, we are not at peace with ourselves.

The secret to attaining a level of peace with ourselves is to be ever aware that God loves us just as we are. He loves us with all our gifts and talents, with all our faults and self-centeredness. We cannot reason ourselves into such a conviction of God's infinite, enduring, personal love for us; we must hear the Lord himself telling us that his love for us is boundless.

The Lord speaks to our hearts in the words of Scripture. How convincingly he tells us: "Fear not, for I have redeemed you; I have called you by name: you are mine.... you are precious in my eyes, and honored, and I love you" (Is 43:1, 4). When any anxiety about our sinfulness plagues us, we are assured: "'My steadfast love shall not depart from you, and my covenant of peace shall not be removed,' says the Lord, who has compassion on you" (Is 54:10). How comforting are the words of Jesus: "As the Father has loved me, so have I loved you. Abide in my love" (Jn 15:9). We know that the Father's love for Jesus is infinite, and Jesus assures us that his love for us is also unconditional and unchanging.

Mary was certainly aware of the Lord's infinite love which enabled her to be at peace with herself come what may. As our loving, caring Mother who is aware of our difficulties in this area, Mary will help us to experience that same peaceful self-acceptance.

Peace with Others

Scripture does not say anythng directly about Mary's experience in this area. From our little glimpses into her life, however, we can glean a few insights that point to Mary's peaceful relationships with other people.

Consider the Visitation, for example. As soon as Mary learned that Elizabeth was expecting in her old age, she immediately made the arduous trip to assist her relative at this time. From a human perspective, these two women had little in common. Elizabeth was elderly and belonged to the priestly class, the wealthy class of Judea at that time. Mary was a young woman, poor and with little or no social status. Yet Mary and Elizabeth enjoyed a happy, peaceful relationship because the Lord and his miraculous workings were the focal point in their lives. As they prayed and praised God together, their relationship grew much stronger; such is the bonding power of prayer.

We can certainly picture Mary as a good neighbor in Nazareth, quietly radiating the presence of the Lord wherever she went. Mary also mingled with the other women who followed Jesus as he went about his ministry. How much they must have benefited from her presence!

Without a doubt, Mary was loved and appreciated by the disciples her son had chosen and upon whom he founded his kingdom. Her presence with them in the Upper Room after the Ascension testifies to her close relationship with them: "All these with one accord devoted themselves to prayer, together with the women and Mary, the Mother of Jesus, and with his brethren" (Acts 1:14).

How to Love Your Neighbor

Jesus gave us a very brief but vitally important directive on how to attain a peaceful relationship with others: "You shall love your neighbor as yourself" (Mt 22:39). Of course, we cannot do this without first being at peace with God and with ourselves. Having made progress in these first two areas, we can then move on.

If we expect others to love and accept us, with all our idiosyncrasies, it is equally important for us to accept and love others.

Like ourselves, each person we meet is the sum total of all their life's experiences. We cannot possibly know what has gone into molding and forming them into the person they are today. How, then, can we sit in judgment on them and their conduct?

Our own insecurity may prompt us to be critical or judgmental at times, without our fully realizing that what we judge as a fault in another person is probably a reflection of our own shortcoming. To avoid being critical and judgmental we need to develop a positive attitude which sees the good qualities in every person, since every person is a special creation of God. Those who are responsible for the physical and spiritual welfare of others, such as parents, teachers, and pastors, clearly have an obligation to admonish a wayward person. However, the intention of the person making such a correction distinguishes him or her from those who are merely being critical.

Mary, our Queen of Peace, would remind us that we all belong to the family of God. Through baptism we have been born into the Kingdom of God, and as we follow the way of Christ we become full-fledged members of the Body of Christ.

The Lord loves every person with an unbounded love, as he loves us. We manifest our love and appreciation of his love for us by loving our neighbor as ourselves. In striving to do so, we will enjoy peace within ourselves and be at peace with all the other special friends of God.

Peace with Creation

Being at peace with creation encompasses our acceptance of every aspect of creation: the beauty and majesty of the created world and everything in it—including ourselves, with all our God-given endowments and also the limitations and weaknesses imposed by our humanness.

Mary's life gives evidence that she had attained this level of peace with creation. When she beheld the beauty of God's created world, she rejoiced as she sang those magnificent psalms which extol his handiwork. Mary found great peace and joy in God's plan for motherhood and in her own unique motherhood. She was at peace because she knew that she was loved and appreciated. She knew that she had been chosen for her special vocation because God loved her with an infinite love. This was the source of her peace—and can be the source of ours as well.

Our Queen of Peace also experienced peace in the limitations imposed upon us as creatures. The long, exhausting journey to Bethlehem must have been an ordeal for a pregnant woman, but Mary made it quietly and peacefully, recognizing that this was all in God's plan. With a heavy but peaceful heart, she accepted the fatigue and hardships of the flight to Egypt in order to save her child from Herod's murderous plans. Amid the privations of poverty and the rigors of her household duties, Mary was at peace, since the Prince of Peace was abiding with her and within her.

Appreciating God's Handiwork

How do we relate to God's creation? As we pause to survey and reflect on the exquisite beauty that surrounds us, we will be at peace, recognizing creation as an expression of divine love. Take time to reflect on the dexterity and adaptability of our five external senses. In the words of one catchy expression, "Take time to stop and smell the roses," to appreciate God's creation all around us. We must also turn that appreciation inward and thank God for his handiwork best expressed by the psalmist: "I give you thanks that I am fearfully and wonderfully made...." (Ps 139:14, NRSV).

More difficult may be the peaceful acceptance of limitations imposed on us by illness, fatigue, advanced age, lack of talent, or the means to accomplish our heart's desire. In creating us, God endowed each of us with all the spiritual and temporal gifts we would need to fulfill our mission in life and enable us to reach our eternal salvation. People burdened with disabilities and limitations—spiritual, physical, or emotional—are participating in God's mysterious plan. In the same way, those who care for a disadvantaged person are fulfilling the Lord's command to love: "As you did it to one of the least of these my brethren, you did it to me" (Mt 25:40).

Despite our limitations and shortcomings, we can remain at peace if we keep ourselves aware of the sacred writer's reminder: "We know that in everything God works for good with those who love him, who are called according to his purpose" (Rom 8:28).

With the powerful intercession of our Queen of Peace, this awareness will enable us to maintain our peace with every phase of creation.

Emissaries All

Mary's intercession for us and her presentation of the Prince of Peace are intended to make a change in the way we live. Through the Queen of Peace Jesus calls us not only to live his way of peace but also to become peacemakers—by radiating his love, peace, and joy through our attitudes and actions. Jesus even proclaimed a special Beatitude for all those who would strive to attain inner peace and then reflect genuine peace to every person who crosses their path: "Blessed are the peacemakers for they will be called sons of God" (Mt 5:9).

Each time we participate in the sacrifice of the Mass, we are offering the most powerful prayer for peace. And at the conclusion of every Mass, we are commissioned to be peacemakers to every person we meet. Each of the three suggested ending commissions of the Mass is brief but direct:

"Go in the peace of Christ."

"The Mass is ended, go in peace."

"Go in peace to love and serve the Lord."

May the Queen of Peace, the guiding Star of the millennial renewal, lead us to Jesus, who is the source of true peace. And through Mary's intercession, may we in turn present Jesus to others and become effective ambassadors of his peace.

If we were to summarize the message of this book into one sentence, it might read something like this:

> Mary, the Mother of Jesus and our Mother, is the Guiding Star who leads us into the millennial renewal by urging us to develop a personal relationship with Jesus, to be docile to the inspirations and guidance of the Holy Spirit, and to make our pilgrimage to the Father a journey of loving response to his unconditional love for us.

Mary's whole lifestyle charts the course for us in all phases of the renewal. In her own life Mary put into practice all the primary objectives of the expected renewal. Her example enkindles within us "a true longing for holiness, a deep desire for...personal renewal in a context of ever more intense prayer." From this will flow our "solidarity with one's neighbor, especially the most needy." [1]

Mary's lifestyle is an ideal model for our emulation. She not only shows us the way, but, as our Guiding Star, she accompanies us in all three stages of preparation.

In the first year of preparation (1997), our whole focus is on the Person of Jesus as we strive to know him with our heart. We will also contemplate Mary, in the words of Pope John Paul II, "especially in the mystery of her Divine Motherhood.... Mary in fact constantly points to her Divine Son and she is proposed to all believers as the model of faith which is put into practice." [2]

In the second phase of preparation (1998), our Holy Father calls us to "a renewed appreciation of the presence and activity of the Spirit" in our lives.[3] Here again Mary is our exemplar. Throughout her whole life she was guided by the interior activity of the Holy Spirit. In this stage of preparation, we will contemplate and imitate her "as a woman who was docile to the voice of the Spirit, a woman of silence and attentiveness, a woman of hope."[4] Our contemplation will bring us to a deeper appreciation of the activity of the Holy Spirit, dynamic and operative within us since the time of our baptism.

In the final year of preparation (1999), Mary's immense love for the Father will increase our own love for Him. "The whole of Christian life is like a great pilgrimage to the house of the Father," writes Pope John Paul II.[5] As we journey we become more aware of his unconditional love for each one of us.

As we proceed prayerfully and reflectively through these pages, with Mary as our Guiding Star and with the assistance of God's grace, we will be better prepared to fulfill our role in the Great Renewal we are eagerly anticipating.

As we reflect on Mary's mission to be the Mother of the Messiah, to nurture and care for him in his early years, we can better appreciate her ongoing mission to our world today. As our spiritual Mother, Mary is deeply concerned about the success of the universal conversion to which we have been called as we enter the third millennium.

In these days of the millennial renewal, Pope John Paul II put complete faith and trust in Mary's powerful intercession when he placed the whole mission under her patronage in the closing paragraph of his apostolic letter:

I entrust this responsibility of the whole Church to the maternal intercession of Mary, Mother of the Redeemer. She, the Mother of Fairest Love, will be for Christians on the way to the Great Jubilee of the Third Millennium the Star which safely guides their steps to the Lord. May the unassuming Young

Woman of Nazareth, who two thousand years ago offered to the world the Incarnate Word, lead the men and women of the new millennium towards the One who is "the true light that enlightens every man (Jn 1:9)."[6]

Notes

Introduction

1. *Tertio Millennio Adveniente*, par. 43.
2. *Tertio Millennio Adveniente*, par. 44.
3. *Tertio Millennio Adveniente*, par. 48.
4. *Tertio Millennio Adveniente*, par. 45.
5. *Tertio Millennio Adveniente*, par. 54.

ONE
Mary, Guiding Star of the New Millennium

1. Francis P. LeBuffe, S.J., *The Hound of Heaven: An Interpretation* (New York: Macmillan, 1949) lines 1-5.
2. Pope John Paul II, *Crossing the Threshold of Hope* (New York: Alfred A. Knopf, Inc., 1994) 103-04.
3. *Tertio Millennio Adveniente*, par. 18.
4. *Tertio Millennio Adveniente*, par. 26.
5. *Tertio Millennio Adveniente*, par. 42.
6. *Tertio Millennio Adveniente*, par. 42.

TWO
Guadalupe: A Call to Build a Community of Faith

1. *Tertio Millenio Adveniente*, par. 42.

THREE
Lourdes: A Call to Healing and Holiness

1. *Catechism of the Catholic Church*, par. 491.
2. Fr. J. Leo Boyle, *The Story of Lourdes* (New York: Paulist Press, 1949).
3. *Lumen Gentium*, par. 42.
4. *Tertio Millennio Adveniente*, par. 42.

FIVE
Medjugorje: A Call to the Sacramental Life

1. *Tertio Millennio Adveniente*, par. 50.
2. *Tertio Millennio Adveniente*, par. 55.

SIX
Mary, Mother of the Church

1. *Catechism of the Catholic Church*, par. 963.

SEVEN
Mary: Model of Discernment and Obedience

1. *Tertio Millennio Adveniente*, par. 42.
2. *Tertio Millennio Adveniente*, par. 42.
3. *Tertio Millennio Adveniente*, par. 48.
4. *Lumen Gentium*, par. 56.

EIGHT
Mary: Model of Prayer

1. *Tertio Millennio Adveniente*, par. 40.
2. Sister Wendy Mary Beckett, "Simple Prayer," *The Clergy Review*, 1978.

NINE
Mary: Model of Faith and Hope

1. *Tertio Millennio Adveniente*, par. 42.
2. *Catechism of the Catholic Church*, par. 1817.
3. *Catechism of the Catholic Church*, par. 1843.
4. *Lumen Gentium*, par. 68.
5. *Tertio Millennio Adveniente*, par. 48.

TEN
Mary: Model of Suffering

1. *Tertio Millennio Adveniente*, par. 42.

ELEVEN
Mary: Model of Discipleship

1. Fr. Carroll Stuhlmuller, C.P., *The Jerome Biblical Commentary*, 145.
2. St. Augustine, Sermon 25 presentation.
3. Fr. John L. McKenzie, S.J., *The Jerome Biblical Commentary*, 86.
4. *Catechism of the Catholic Church*, par. 654.
5. "Spiritual Exercises of St. Ignatius."
6. *Tertio Millennio Adveniente*, par. 45.
7. *Tertio Millennio Adveniente*, par. 49.

TWELVE
Mary: Queen of Peace

1. *Catechism of the Catholic Church*, par. 974.
2. *Acta Apostolica Sedes* 42 (1950), par. 760-62, 767-69.
3. "Dogmatic Constitution on the Church," *Lumen Gentium*, par. 62.
4. *Lumen Gentium*, par. 62.
5. *Lumen Gentium*, par. 65.

Epilogue

1. *Tertio Millennio Adveniente*, 42.
2. *Tertio Millennio Adveniente*, 43.
3. *Tertio Millennio Adveniente*, 45.
4. *Tertio Millennio Adveniente*, 48.
5. *Tertio Millennio Adveniente*, 49.
6. *Tertio Millennio Adveniente*, 59.